# YOUR HIDDEN ASSETS
## The key to getting executive jobs

# YOUR HIDDEN ASSETS
## The key to getting executive jobs

Orrin G. Wood, Jr.

Dow Jones-Irwin
Homewood, Illinois 60430

© DOW JONES-IRWIN, 1982

ISBN 0-87094-266-2
Library of Congress Catalog Card No. 81-67116
*Printed in the United States of America*

1 2 3 4 5 6 7 8 9 0 K 9 8 7 6 5 4 3 2

**TO JOAN**

*Whose support and encouragement over the years
have helped make this book a reality.*

# PREFACE

This book is written for all executives—men and women—who are looking for a job or thinking about it. It is especially for you who are at or nearing mid-career.

What is the need for another book in this field when there are already a great many? First of all, only a couple of them have tried to address the variety and complexity of problems executives face in a job search. Second, in my feedback as a counselor for more than a decade I have repeatedly been told by successful job hunters that most books on the subject are too superficial. *Your Hidden Assets* goes beyond generalities into the specifics that the best counselors use working with their clients—and in the process it will help you sharpen your job-hunting skills.

What are the job-hunting skills I'm talking about? Some of them are what you have developed in past jobs—but some are quite different!

To name a few: *determining your principal priorities in a job, selling yourself, dealing with trauma, managing your time productively,* and *evaluating offers.*

What are my qualifications for writing such a book?

At age 45, I conducted a six-month job campaign which resulted in interviews for 52 actual jobs and five offers, all roughly comparable to my former one as a treasurer of a nationally known company. Almost all these interviews were for jobs within commuting distance of my home. The most important thing that happened in my job search was the improvement of my job-hunting skills.

I was a cofounder and am currently a counselor in a job counseling workshop run by the Boston chapter of the Harvard Business School Alumni Association. In the last 10 years this program has served more than 1,000 people, mostly alumni. It has become a key element in a growing network of counseling services in the Boston area.

My role as a volunteer counselor of well over 500 men and women has evolved more and more into channeling them into the best sources of help (volunteer as well as professional) available.

I have put extensive effort into getting feedback from those I have counseled. This has given me good insight into the wide range of problems many job hunters have had and the most effective techniques they have used to cope with them.

To show how *Your Hidden Assets* gives much more thorough instructions in helping you develop job-hunting skills, consider the process of preparing a resume. The vast majority of executive job-hunting books stress the importance of a resume. But they devote little attention to instructing you how to analyze your *background* in the detail necessary to prepare a top-flight one. Here are some of the unique steps that are described in this book:

1. *Determining your job requirements:* how to define your most important job considerations and their priority: that is, the specific responsibilities, the type of environment, the financial aspects, future prospects, and the kind of life you want to lead.
2. *Analyzing what an employer is looking for:* how to identify what an employer is looking for (skills and personal attributes) and what weaknesses he or she wants to avoid.
3. *Determining what you have to offer:* how to develop the most extensive list of your knowledge and experience so they can be used to show a variety of skills and personal traits, and how to defuse any deficiencies you have.
4. *Preparing a strong resume:* what type of resume to use; how to analyze your background for the three or four principal assets that you will want to emphasize; and how to identify the best people to evaluate your resume.

Instructions on all other aspects of a campaign are just as thorough. The Table of Contents explains the wide variety of problems that are included.

Hundreds of people have contributed ideas to this book; the vast majority are successful job hunters who have given me feedback on their campaigns. Also included have been several dozen employment professionals. The contributions of two counselors stand out: Lee Wotherspoon, a psychologist, whose detailed editing and various ideas have been very important; and Neil S. MacKenna, President of Career Assistance, Inc., who gave me great help in my job campaign and who played a major role in the HBSAB workshop and in evaluating this book. Others whose ideas have been important are:

Allen N. Clapp, Senior Vice President
Spencer Stuart & Associates

Rawle Deland, Partner
Thorndike Deland Associates; former president
of the Association of Executive Recruiting
Consultants, Inc.

Ms. Alice C. Early, Former Director of Alumni
Placement, Harvard Business School; currently
Associate, Russell Reynolds Associates, Inc.

John G. Eresian, Cofounder of Harvard Business
School Association of Boston Job Counseling
Program

Ray P. Foote, Jr., Vice President
Heidrick & Struggles, Inc.

John T. Goodhue, Chairman
The Man Marketing Clinic of Sales Executive
Club of New York

Barrie S. Greiff, M.D., Psychiatrist,
Harvard Business School, who designed and
teaches the School's Executive Family Seminar

W. James Parker, Chairman of the Board
Parker, Eldridge, Sholl & Gordon

John E. Steele, Former Director of Placement
Harvard Business School; currently Career
Planning and Placement Center Director, Boston College

Timothy M. Warren, Morton Baker, and Tristam A.
Coffin have been most helpful also; as has been
Rosalie K. Crosby of Girl Friday Associates.

Orrin G. Wood, Jr.

# CONTENTS

# Chapter one

# PUTTING THINGS IN PERSPECTIVE

**You're out of a job**

Here you are, a manager in mid-career, and you're out of work.

Maybe business in general has been poor, and cutbacks were in order. You didn't survive all the cuts.

Or maybe the company was simply going down the drain because top management chose to stick with buggy whips when it should have switched to transmissions.

Perhaps you're the victim of a sale or merger. The people now on top want their own teams, and for any number of reasons that does not include you.

Regardless of the reason for your firing, you're part of a sizable army. According to *Business Week:* "Even in rosy times, it's estimated that about 500,000 managers are fired each year. It happens on all levels, and it happens for a wide variety of reasons, some of which aren't very rational."

Or you may be on a job and about to tell your boss, "Take this job and shove it!"

For whatever reason, you have a crisis in your career, and this book aims to help you. First we discuss attitudes, and next look at some traps you can fall into. Then we move on to details.

**Accent the positive**

What kind of people do you respond to most favorably on first meeting? The pessimists, the grumblers—or those who are cheerful, positive, and enthusiastic? And so it is with job hunters.

Starting off on the right foot is terribly important, and the impressions you make on possible employers in the first few minutes of meeting are crucial. Not that a favorable impression at the start will necessarily carry through even the first interview or the series of interviews it may take to get a new job, but a negative attitude will often ruin your chances in the first five or ten minutes. Psyching yourself up to make every interview a success will help you display a positive attitude.

Not only is a positive attitude important with prospective employers, it is also important in dealing with your friends. If you display a negative attitude with them, it will convince them it was your fault that things didn't work out for you at XYZ, and they may not stretch themselves to give you more than perfunctory help. Obviously you want the help of as many people as possible—and their best help—at this time. Furthermore, a negative attitude will cause you real difficulties in any job you get.

How can you avoid such an attitude? Analyze the things that you have to be thankful for, and develop a positive image of yourself through careful preparation of your credentials for your job search. These steps will give your confidence a real lift.

Another key step is to carry on an aggressive campaign. You should be so busy that you have little time for negative feelings, and you will always have some positive prospects ahead of you.

**You have a lot going for you**

Being out of a job is distressing, yet a job search also gives you a chance to reflect on the important and positive aspects of your life. This may be your opportunity to find a job more in line with your current and future needs.

But you may ask, "Just what do I really have to be thankful for?"

Before you answer this question visualize yourself six months or a year from now, when you have accepted the kind of job you really want and are working again. You are getting a good salary. Your life is settled in a normal routine. You have the prestige among your friends and in your community that comes from having a job considered a good one. You are dealing daily with interesting people and can use your skills and experience to solve challenging problems. These are your goals, your expectations. Now look at some other items that might be going for you.

Your health—if you have good health, you have one of the greatest assets in the world. You may not be in the best of health, but take a look around you and realize how much better off you are than many.

Your family—if you have a strong family, it is one of the most satisfying things in life and can be a great source of comfort and pleasure. At this time you likely will be very pleased by the support your family gives you.

Your friends—you have a great many of them, more than you probably realize. Most of them stand ready to help in any way possible. Often they will not seek you out, since they don't know how they can help. You will be pleased how most of them will support you, if you contact them.

The positive accomplishments in your career and your life—not only is this important background for your campaign, but it is a source of great strength for you. The careful preparation plan explained later will help you recognize all you have to offer.

Your material possessions—they are a means for you to lead a reasonably comfortable life, and are a source of satisfaction and pleasure.

No one wants to go through a job search at this time in life, but the process can provide opportunity. First of all, you have a chance to find out what's important for you in a job and a good chance of finding one that really fits you. Second, you will be exposed to a world of work that is much wider than you ever imagined. Out of this can come a job that is tailored to your current strengths and interests. Third, to be successful in a job campaign you will need to sharpen management tools that may have become rusty, but that can be valuable in the future. And finally, your job search will find you a number of new friends—some of them for life.

**Getting things in focus**

A lot of people have been through a job search that ended well. Today it's your turn—tomorrow it will be somebody else's. What you are going through is temporary—several years from now it will seem like a dim memory. In terms of your whole career, a job search really is just a short, passing phase.

You've conquered lots of obstacles in the past. Many of the times which have given you the most satisfaction have been when you have faced a tough problem and licked it. You will have a lot of satisfaction looking back at your job search five years from now, when you can say, "I licked that problem, too."

Being out of work might make you uncomfortable among people, both in your search and socially. That's normal. Very likely though you're concentrating on what you consider the stigma of your current situation. If you conduct an effective search and are optimistic about the outcome, your upset will amount to little.

Sure you will have disappointments. That's part of the process. But there will also be a number of rewards. People will rally to support you—often people you don't know or hardly know—and this will be a source of real satisfaction.

There are three alternatives for you: One, you can withdraw, or withdraw in effect by running a low-key campaign and hoping that somebody will rescue you. Two, you can run a campaign with little emotional risk—mailing hundreds of resumes to companies, answering ads, and concentrating on seeing your friends. This is considerably better than the first, but it underplays the opportunity you have. Three, you can show the world what you are really made of. You can work hard, you can take a lot of emotional risk, you can be really critical about your attitudes and your biases. What kind of campaign are you going to run?

**A word about being fired**

But what if you've been fired? It's hard to be positive about that, you say. Hard, perhaps. Impossible, no.

Being fired usually sets a person off on a gamut of emotions, beginning with surprise, even shock, and moving to chagrin, anger, and bitterness. A person feels guilty, unwanted, a failure. Unless you're different from most people, you've had those feelings descend on you. Just don't let them drive you to self pity and apathy.

Flip back and read that quote from *Business*

*Week* again. If you've been fired, you belong to the most unexclusive club in the world. And because of sheer numbers, if for no other reason, there's little stigma attached to being fired.

One word of caution, though. Don't rush out and take any old job just to show your former boss and company. Contrary to myth, few people are fired for incompetency. And that makes sense, for to fire a person for that reason simply demonstrates a boss's own incompetency—faulty judgment for hiring that person or poor supervision.

A person is fired mainly because of a change in management or the fact that the company or one of its programs is doing badly. Sometimes a boss doesn't like a particular employee, for whatever reason. And that person probably doesn't like the boss, either.

So take heart. You're not incompetent. Simply put, you were in the wrong job at the wrong time. And now you have a chance to find one that's right.

*Getting what's yours*

If you're fired, the first thing to do is negotiate the best deal possible for yourself. You're in the strongest position to do this at the firing interview. The person conducting this interview is often inexperienced, feels guilty, and is unsure of him/herself. (Often they are as much to blame for the firing as you are.) If your company does not have clear-cut policies on separations, you can drive a harder bargain. The key things to negotiate are as follows:

*1. An outplacement service.* Your first priority is to get another top job, and you should use the best resources possible to do this. If you are over 40, demand that the company sponsor you and pay for a top-flight service of this type (the name of the service to be approved by you). Such a service is commonly offered by many well-run companies. If the company will not pay the fee, make sure they will at least sponsor you.

*2. Severance pay.* Many companies don't really know what they should pay. What constitutes a reasonable amount depends on your length of service, your position within the company, and its policy. Try to get at least one month's pay for every year of service, with a minimum of 3 months. Make sure that you will have the right to a reasonable extension, if necessary.

*3. Office space and a part-time secretary.* This can be an extremely useful service.

*4. Unemployment insurance.* Make sure that the arrangements are made so that you will qualify, if you choose.

*5. Group insurance coverage.* Request that this coverage be extended to you (at the company's expense) until you get relocated.

*6. References.* Get clear agreement on the reason the company will give for your leaving and the kind of reference they will give you.

Now let's look at the traps that may be in your path.

# Chapter two

# AVOID TRAPS

**No vacation— yet**

The temptation to put off beginning a job search is great. Maybe you've dreamed about an extended vacation. And once you find a job, you can't expect ordinary vacation time for at least a year. Besides, you have severance pay.

Resist the temptation. Promise yourself time off once you've landed a job, before beginning work. If you delay a start, you'll soon realize that you've wasted a lot of valuable time as well as financial resources.

When athletes get out of shape, they must work hard and long to get back into it—and performance suffers in the interim. Right now you're in good trim—geared to working under pressure and meeting deadlines. So keep momentum going by swinging immediately into your job search. Don't fall into the "I deserve a vacation" trap.

**Six months' notice?**

Perhaps you have six months before you must leave your company. Your boss has said that you might conduct your job search on company time, although you'll have certain continuing responsibilities. This can work to your advantage—if you use the time effectively.

Six months is a whole half year. Surely you'll find a good job in that time, and what's more you'll be doing useful work. Don't fool yourself.

That six months will go by rapidly, and your first priority is to get another job. Do what you need to do for the company, but use as close to 100 percent of your time on your job search as you can manage. Don't cut back on your efforts until the company complains.

## Consulting— maybe

You may think you can do some consulting work temporarily, instead of looking right away for a new position. This holds numerous hazards.

To be sure, you earn income and you stay in shape. Consulting might lead to a permanent job.

But time passes and job-hunting inertia sets in— and that's hard to overcome. Earning income, while important, isn't your number one goal. If you do consult, seize every opportunity to look for a job. Don't put much stock in the idea that consulting itself will become your permanent occupation. The odds against consulting leading to a good job are high.

## Visible and hidden markets

There are two job markets. One is visible, the other hidden. Don't fall into the trap of concentrating wholly on the first.

The Sunday *New York Times* and *The Wall Street Journal* carry pages of advertisements for executive jobs. The classified directories of any metropolitan area contain lists of employment agencies and executive recruiters. Ads and lists relate to the *visible* job market—*known* jobs that companies want to fill.

Employment agencies and recruiters stay in business by locating employees for key jobs—the kind you're seeking. To focus on them as well as on ads would be normal. Yet if you concentrate wholly on the visible, you entrap yourself. The *hidden* market contains fully three quarters of all jobs available. This is the market in which job hunters must find and make contact with executives who are not actively seeking candidates, but *are* in a position to hire.

The "Sources of Management Jobs" chart, Table 2-1, breaks down the market into visible and hidden and shows the characteristics of each.

Newspaper ads, employment agencies, and recruiters cast a wide net, which pulls in a host of candidates. Competition for known jobs is fierce. The visible market is overrun with "elite" candidates—the younger, well-trained, and desirable who stand out in a crowd. This pool diminishes with age

**TABLE 2-1**
**Sources of management jobs**

|  | *Source* | *Characteristics* | *Candidates selected* |
|---|---|---|---|
| Visible market (25% of all jobs) | Ads<br>Executive recruiters<br>Consultants<br>CPAs<br>Employment agencies<br>Personnel departments<br>Banks<br>Trade associations | Active search by employer<br>Screening by an intermediary<br>Tight specifications<br>Easy to apply for (letter plus resume)<br>Highly competitive | Specialists (usually with directly related experience)<br>Among best of peers<br>"The elite" |
| Hidden market (75% of all jobs) | Approaching a key executive directly | Passive (if any search)<br>Screening by key executive<br>Flexible specifications<br>Getting interview requires aggressive approach (referrals, direct contact)<br>Little competition<br>Often job is created | Often:<br>Executive with reasonable record who appears compatible<br>Can be:<br>"The rest of us" |

(even for those with highly marketable skills) as Table 2-2 indicates. But for a person in mid-career, it's a tough group to buck. As an older, experienced executive, your chances are much better in the hidden market, where positions are more plentiful and competition is less.

You'll use every resource available to land the job you want. You'll answer ads and you'll work with agencies and executive recruiters. But ignore the hidden market at your peril—more about this later.

**TABLE 2-2**
**Your marketability**

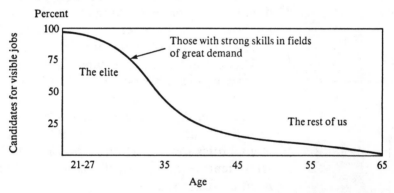

**Help from employment professionals**
You may have sought expert aid on a number of occasions to help you solve various problems on the job. You may have hired a consultant to help with a complicated problem. In your personal life, you probably have called on specialists—a doctor, a lawyer, a banker, or a tax expert. All have plenty of competent professionals. Expert job counseling is limited, but if you can find it, it may well make a substantial difference in the number and type of opportunities you'll be offered. So try to find it. If you can, it can be well worth it. And often you can find good counseling for a reasonable fee. I

have seen dozens of job hunters who with the help of good in-depth counseling have changed faltering job searches into successful ones. Others have entrapped themselves by ignoring counseling opportunities.

**Executive recruiters and employment agencies**

Don't expect job counseling from executive recruiters and employment agencies. These people seek candidates for specialized jobs. Since their success depends on satisfying rigid employer specifications and because they work under great pressure, they have little time to counsel you unless you have a high potential for filling the kinds of jobs they handle. Their skill lies in evaluating candidates for employers, not in counseling candidates on how to be more effective in the job-hunting process (the kind of help you may need).

This doesn't mean you shouldn't see all the recruiters you can. You should—provided it does not distract you from approaching the hidden market. Listen carefully to the recruiter's advice, but be realistic about it. A chart of the "Roles of Employment Professionals" is shown in Table 2-3. Counselors represent only a small fraction of all employment professionals.

**Counselors**

The availability of effective professional counseling help is further limited by the fact that many of the best, even for the high fees that they often charge, are not available to most job seekers. Generally the most skillful are the outplacement specialists, a category that developed recently after employers accepted responsibility for placing those people they let go in other jobs. Outplacement specialists work for the employer laying off personnel. The fact that outplacement specialists will sometimes spend 50 to 100 hours working with a job seeker gives some idea of the in-depth counseling they can provide.

**TABLE 2-3**
Roles of employment professionals (a rough guide)

| | Type of firm | Services provided | Range of salary | Fee | Who pays fee | Job search counseling given |
|---|---|---|---|---|---|---|
| Recruitment | Executive recruiters Management consultants CPAs (financial jobs) | Thorough search for outstanding candidates for senior jobs | Over $40,000 | 30% of annual salary | Employer | Little |
| | Employment agencies | Superficial screening for lower-level jobs | Under $40,000 | 15% of annual salary | Employer | Little |
| Counseling | Outplacement specialists | Counseling of job hunter on all phases of a campaign, your "campaign manager," up to 100 hours of individual counseling | Usually over $30,000 | 15% of annual salary, usually a flat fee | Past employer | Extensive |
| | Job counselors, career counselors | Similar to outplacement (but much less intensive) | Any | 1-10% of annual salary, can be hourly fee | Job hunter | Considerable |
| | Vocational counselors | Tests and counsels on career choice | Any | $100-$300 | Job hunter | Little |
| Matching and counseling | College and trade associations | Matching of available people and jobs, with referral of good candidates to employers | Any alumnus or member | Token if any | Job hunter | Little |

If your former company does not provide outplacement service, you might obtain it on your
own. Use *The Directory of Outplacement Firms—
1980* (Consultant News, Templeton Road, Fitzwilliam, N.H. 03447), to locate one in your area.
If the firm insists on company sponsorship, try to
get your former company to sponsor you and pay
the fee. If the company won't pay the fee, it will
probably at least sponsor you—that way you can
become a client provided you pay the fee. You
can also be sponsored by a friend who is a former
client or someone who works for a company that
has used the service. Ask for references from the
outplacement firm(s) you're interested in and seek
references on your own. Executive recruiters, personnel managers, and workshop counselors should
be sources for such references.

Try to work with a counseling service on an
hourly fee, if possible. You may be able to negotiate a fee to cover only the services you need.
Many people have received excellent counseling for
less than $1,000. If the directory doesn't provide
you with the name of a service to meet your needs,
ask employment professionals and counselors if
they know of a good one.

I urge you also not to overlook volunteer counseling services for established professionals. Though
they are few in number, some of them are very
good. Other possible sources of help include management consultants, CPAs for financial jobs, and
job, career, and vocational counselors.

**Spoiling your**     What about friends and other personal contacts?
**best contacts**     Let's see.

"Tom, if there's anything I can do for you, let
me know. We are always looking for people with a
lot on the ball like you," said Frank, Tom's regular
golfing buddy and senior vice president of the biggest bank in town. So when Tom lost his job two
years later, Frank was the first person he called. A

lunch at the city's most exclusive club resulted. Frank gave Tom lots of encouragement but explained that there weren't any suitable openings at the bank just then. Frank, however, arranged interviews for Tom with three top people in businesses similar to that of Tom's last company. Unfortunately, each in turn resulted in an unsatisfactory interview. Frank was cordial to Tom's follow-up call, but he only gave Tom a couple of lukewarm suggestions. These proved to be even less fruitful than the first contacts. Tom's subsequent calls to Frank went unanswered.

Tom's experience with Frank is typical of what happens with contacts if you don't handle them properly. Influential contacts can be a great help, but regardless of the closeness of your friendship, don't expect important people to jeopardize their reputations with their professional peers unless they feel you are going to be a good representative. Nor are they likely to give you a second chance. When people have come to you for help in the past, haven't you been pretty selective about whom you have referred them to?

A contact can't make a favorable impression for you—you have to do that yourself. You may have a few friends who want to open influential doors for you, so it is essential to get your preparation done quickly.

The key to getting the best effort from influential contacts is making the most favorable impression on them. Past or social relationships may not mean a great deal. So you should be prepared to make the most favorable impression possible when you see your influential contacts.

**Blindly accepting advice from friends**

Naturally you are anxious to seek out your friends in the most responsible positions, because not only may they be able to offer you a job, but they likely have the most useful contacts. This makes sense, but it can also be a trap.

Because they are successful, you may think that their advice will be excellent. It may be. Unfortunately for you, though, many of these successful executives may have achieved their success without ever having been exposed to the job market from a job-hunter's standpoint. So they may have little understanding of what you need.

In addition, friends usually do not want to hurt your feelings, and say nothing even though they may think you make a poor impression. Therefore, they may tell you what they think you want to hear, rather than what you should hear. Actually the friends who are critical (provided it's constructive criticism) may be doing you a big favor. Early in your interviews with friends, make clear that you understand that they may be reluctant to be critical, but that candor may be most useful to you.

Most people—especially your friends—want to help you. Some will approach you. Most won't know how to help—and won't volunteer—but they will respond willingly if you contact them. More than likely, few of these people can help you de velop your job-hunting skills (probably your greatest need), but they can be invaluable in providing contacts. It's up to you to decide who is likely to be most helpful and to ask them specifically for this help. You may be surprised to find that some of the people you would least expect to help may be the most useful.

**Being overly optimistic**

You probably have a good record. You may have friends in responsible positions. You may have put on an aggressive campaign to date. You may have had a few interviews and had several people say they are working on something for you. You also may have an interview coming up in a couple of days and another possibility next week. Even though nothing definite has developed yet, you are quite confident that things are going well for you.

Don't kid yourself, for you may be in a trap.

You probably only scratched the surface. It's easy to be deluded into thinking you are doing well. You may be. But what if you aren't? Adopt the attitude that nothing you have started so far is going to work out. Then exert yourself as aggressively as possible to get a new job. Working as hard as you can at your campaign and taking nothing for granted are two of the keys to a successful job search.

**All eggs in one basket**

You may have run into a job possibility that looks ideal, and you have decided to put all your energies into landing it. Be careful, because a situation that looks as though it might jell in two weeks often might not materialize for a month or more, or never. Or if the opportunity does come through, it might be less satisfactory than you thought it would.

Pursuing one opportunity exclusively can be dangerously entrapping. If it doesn't work out, not only will you have wasted a lot of time, but you will also have lost the momentum of your campaign. Make a number of new contacts with possible employers every day. Even when the "ideal" job is about to be offered to you, you may run into something that is even better.

**Working inefficiently**

Because of the amount of work job hunting can entail, how effectively you're organized can make a lot of difference. You'll be working in a "foreign" environment. You might not have anyone to help you with the details (take phone messages, type letters, do your filing and record keeping). Low productivity in this area can greatly hamper your search.

Your routine will involve writing letters you hope will bring interviews, answering ads, doing research (on companies, industries, and individuals), phoning (for interviews, information, and following up), and interviews (for actual jobs, for information, and for referrals). Your principal needs are a place to work, a phone, someone to take phone messages, and a typist. Find a base other than your home—it's too distracting. Depending on circumstances, maybe your former employer might let you use an office. Ask for it. As a second choice, try to get office space from a friend—a professional or someone who runs a small business (all you really need is a desk and access to a phone). A less desirable alternative is a library. Actually you'll need a library with good business services for research—and it's a quiet place to work. But if you have to use pay phones, make sure the operator won't interrupt—charge toll calls to your home number. Get an answering service or have a friend take phone messages for you.

Don't do your own typing—your time is far more valuable doing things that nobody can do for you. Find a good typist—you'll need that service— and the more you can do with form letters and dictating the better.

The old adage that you have to spend money to make money applies doubly to job hunting because each day's pay lost far exceeds the costs of services you may have to pay for. Outside salespeople are experts at operating in this kind of environment—their tips on working habits, how to get in to see people, and developing effectiveness in interviewing can be helpful. Finally—and this is critical—establish a carefully disciplined work routine and stick to it. Out of the house every day by eight o'clock and home by six. You have no one checking on you. You have no deadlines. Good salespeople learn how to deal with this effectively.

In addition, in all your campaign activities apply the principle of overlapping. The "Overlapping Activities" chart (Table 2-4) shows you how to do this in the preparation of a resume. The "Checklist to Get Started Properly" (Table 2-5) uses these same principles to ensure that your campaign gets off quickly and effectively. After you have read this book, use the checklist to coordinate all your key preparation activities.

TABLE 2-4
Overlapping activities (as applied to preparation of an outstanding resume)

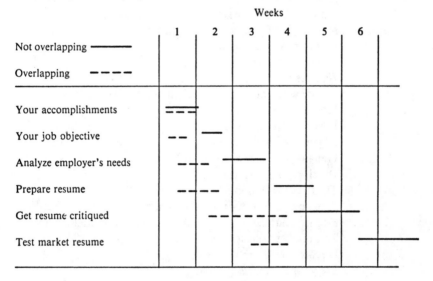

**Don't trap yourself in a mediocre job**

You have already learned that far too many jobs don't work out over a period of time. A key reason for this is that too many job hunters take mediocre jobs because they panic. It is quite easy to make this mistake, particularly when friends urge you to accept a job thinking, as you may be, that you probably won't get a better offer. You can greatly reduce the chances of panic by carefully following the procedures described later for analyzing an

TABLE 2-5
Checklist to get started properly

| Weeks | Step |
|---|---|
| 1-3 | Learn job-hunting techniques and sources of help (study good books; talk to volunteer counselors, recent job hunters; attend seminars). |
| 1 | Line up a good typist. |
| 1 | Get personal stationery (optional). |
| 1 | Apply for unemployment compensation (optional). |
| 1 | Prepare your temporary resume. |
| 1 | Discuss your situation with your family. |
| 1-2 | Line up a place to work outside your house. |
| 1-2 | Line up a place to have your phone answered. |
| 1 | Make a list of your accomplishments. |
| 1 | Write up your accomplishments. |
| 1-2 | Decide on your job objective. |
| 1-2 | Analyze what an employer is most likely to be looking for. |
| 1-2 | Decide who you want to critically evaluate your resume. |
| 1-2 | Prepare your resume (several drafts). |
| 2-3 | Have your resume evaluated. |
| 2-3 | Organize an oral presentation of your accomplishments. |
| 2-3 | Prepare your answers to key questions. |
| 2-3 | Develop your financial plan. |
| 2-3 | Try to get several mock interviews. |
| 3 | Prepare your list of personal contacts. |
| 3 | Prepare your list of key people you want introductions to. |
| 3 | Test market your resume. |
| 3 | Prepare your form letters. |
| 3 | See your references personally. |

offer against your job requirements and for upgrading mediocre offers.

**Watch your financial management**     Having a major reduction in income is a new situation for you. To deal with it, you must be realistic about your finances from the start.

1. Prepare a budget anticipating you'll be out of work for a minimum of six months.

2. If possible, defer the payment of major bills (i.e., mortgage, utilities, etc.). Be candid with your creditors before a crisis comes up. You can also refinance your home or borrow on your life insurance. Try to avoid more drastic steps like selling your home or taking a child out of college—the upset can adversely affect your campaign.

3. Apply for unemployment compensation.

4. Don't short-change your campaign expenses. A revised printing of your resume or an extensive mailing are really fairly cheap in view of the stakes involved.

5. Keep track of your job-hunting expenses—some are tax-deductible.

On the whole, your reduction in income is probably less than you might think, providing you have severance pay and unemployment compensation (which is not taxed), and your federal and state income taxes are lower.

We have seen many of the traps and problems that can arise in a job campaign and how to avoid them. Now let's look at the general principles of a good campaign.

There are 10 principles of job hunting applicable to all and at any time. They are:

1. Often a job hunter goes looking for a job and can't find one—until he or she finds a way to uncover the original source of all jobs—identifying an employer's need that the job hunter can fill.

2. Perhaps a job hunter's greatest assets are knowing what he or she wants to do and having the motivation to find a way to do it.

3. Many employers have certain needs that they will hire to fill (even though they're not actively hiring) if the right candidate comes along.

4. A successful job hunter must get the *serious*

attention of someone in a position to hire—
someone who often has set up defenses to
guard against the superficial approaches of
most job hunters.

5. Effective job hunters are made and not born.
They find good jobs in any economic climate,
while ineffective ones often have great difficulty in even the best of times.

6. Everyone has liabilities, but the skillful job
hunter knows how to sell his or her assets so
that any liabilities are minimized in perspective.

7. An effective job hunter understands an employer's likely needs, what assets have the
greatest appeal to prospective employers, and
how to present them effectively.

8. There are numerous ways to present your credentials—and you may have to experiment with
a number of them to see what works best for
you.

9. Being turned down may present you with a
unique opportunity, if used skillfully, to show
that you are an outstanding candidate.

10. Everything you do in your campaign is judged
as your best.

Now let's see how you choose your preferred
objective—which can be one of the keys to a successful campaign. The remainder of this book aims
to help you here and in other ways.

# Chapter three

# WHAT DO YOU WANT TO DO?

**General principles**

The key to a successful job search is aiming at a job that meets a high percentage of your requirements. This isn't easy because there are a lot of conflicting forces influencing your choice.

For example, "My wife wants me to be president," Sam Rivers, a senior executive, told his friend, a highly respected businessman. This statement tells a lot. Note that this doesn't say, "*I* want to be president." Nor does it say, "My wife wants me to be successful," or "happy," or "challenged"—or even "to earn $100,000." Whether or not this is a logical job requirement for Sam, it was a very important one for him to contend with. Job hunters often make key decisions based more on emotions than on logic—sometimes with dire results. I hope this chapter will help you make your choice more logically.

One of the major activities in your life most comparable to getting a job is deciding on housing. In both, you must establish priorities and evaluate alternatives until you make a choice that meets a high percentage of your priorities. Undoubtedly you will refine your priorities as you search. In buying a residence, for example, you must first decide on housing alternatives (i.e., a condominium, a two- or three-family house, a single-family house, and so on). In a job search, you must decide among career alternatives: first, a career change involving doing something very different from what you've been doing versus doing something similar to what you've been doing; second, which of several alternatives in each category—perhaps buying or starting a business, a job similar to your last one, or consulting. Once you've decided on your preferred career alternative, you must locate and get one or two (or more) offers which meet a high percentage of your priorities and decide which is best for you. Visualize your job search as a two-step process: deciding among career alternatives and then finding the right job.

There are many unhappy job holders who didn't persevere long enough or use good judgment on their last job search. Let me illustrate by telling the story of four job hunters in their 40s, all with advanced degrees from prestigious institutions. One of the four even earned $130,000 a year. All joined well-known companies as members of top management after what appeared to be carefully planned and executed job searches. Two of the job changes involved moving families to a new city. All the jobs failed. Subsequently three of these job hunters reported that they realized on the *first day* of their new jobs that they never should have accepted them. The other realized on the *second day* that the job probably would fail. Can you imagine how a successful executive could make such an error? But these were not exceptions: in my experience perhaps half of the mid-career executives who make a job change are not with the new company five years later. And for an executive making a job

change in mid-career, it seems to me that the minimum time period for success is five years.

William J. Morin, president, director, and chief
executive officer of Drake Beam Morin, Inc., the
largest of the nation's outplacement firms, has
noted the risks involved. He states in the 1980 edition of the *Directory of Outplacement Firms,* a
consultant's news publication, "Many individuals
who are terminated after 5, 10, 15 years with the
company have a tendency to go out, find a job,
and get themselves in trouble very quickly in their
next position. They bounce from that job into the
next job, and they experience this bouncing for a
number of years. This is usually because they did
not take time to ascertain what they did wrong in
the position from which they were first fired and
to honestly determine the proper work environment in which they would be successful."

I do not have to stress that, if you have to go
out on another job search a few years from now, it
probably won't be as easy as this one (hard as this
one may seem). An unsuitable job change at this
stage in your career will make you less marketable. It also will likely be a much greater psychological hurdle, will probably involve less help from
friends, and therefore will mean fewer opportunities. A second change certainly is possible; and
sometimes it is more successful, because the job
hunter is more realistic—but it can be even more
traumatic than what you're going through now.

**At mid-life
your career
tends to
plateau**

In setting your job objective, realize that there's
a pattern to all careers. It's important to identify
where you are and what's probably ahead of you.
The "Phases of Your Career" chart (see Table 3-1)
will be helpful in this.

For example, if you're 38, a desirable job might
be as understudy to an individual who currently

**TABLE 3-1**
Phases of your career

| | General age range | | | |
|---|---|---|---|---|
| | *Early 20s to late 20s* | *Late 20s to early 40s* | *Early 40s to retirement* | *Late 40s/50s to retirement (optional)* |
| Career stage | Early development | Advanced development | Top responsibility | Second career |
| Objective | To identify your career choice and to develop basic skills | To develop in-depth expertise in your field | To utilize your expertise in your major job | To pursue other interests |
| Typical characteristics | 1. Indoctrination into the world of full-time work | 1. Deciding finally on your chosen career (early in this phase) | 1. Your maximum responsibility (perhaps one promotion in the future) | 1. Takes a variety of forms, which are a major change from prior career |
| | 2. Developing basic job skills | 2. Increasing exposure to other company functions through interrelated problems | 2. Often general or administrative management, rather than functional management | 2. A desire to do something you want to do while you can |
| | 3. Broadening your horizons to learn a variety of options for accomplishing your career goal and general requirements for them | 3. Intense pressure to produce and to grow professionally | 3. Broadening of your field of interests on other companies' boards or community committees | 3. Often in much less structured environment so you can pursue other interests (community activities, travel, etc.) |
| | 4. Several promotions | 4. A couple, but less frequent and very important promotions | | 4. Often willing to accept less income (most of cost of raising family over) |
| | 5. Several job changes (often within the same company) | | | 5. Often can arrange so you can pursue second career indefinitely (overcoming fixed retirement age of most companies) |

holds a job that's your ultimate goal. This person might be within five years of retirement or perhaps be a strong candidate for promotion. If you're changing jobs at 50, you might seriously consider a second career or working in a smaller company where your duties would be broader and less structured.

In your 40s and 50s your career may have reached a plateau. In making a job change, you will be in a small minority if you are able to substantially upgrade yourself in terms of salary, responsibilities, and title. You will increase your chances of doing so mainly by joining a high-risk company. But this period in your life presents perhaps one of the few opportunities you will have to make an indepth reassessment of your goals. While it's unlikely that you sought this opportunity, it may come at an opportune time, because your goals and your life in general may be undergoing fundamental change. Throughout your 20s and 30s, your goal may well have been to get "to the top." Maybe in recent years you have recognized the chances of this have become slighter. Or, if your career goal has largely been met, you may feel somewhat at a loss because you don't have a further goal ahead of you. Or you may feel a sense of frustration because achieving the goal has not given you all the personal satisfaction that you had expected.

In any event, you are very likely at a time when the financial demands of your family, because of educational expenses, and so on, are at their peak. There may be upsets because your children are breaking away from home to establish lives of their own. Perhaps your spouse may be employed outside the home, increasing the demands on you at home. It is often a time of great emotional stress. Some of your peers work out their frustrations by drinking too much, playing around, or getting divorced. This is a time to be careful and patient about making a job decision.

The past few years have brought to the forefront a series of studies on the cycles of individuals' lives. Most popularly this is outlined in Gail Sheehy's *Passages*. The central theme in these studies is that most individuals go through a variety of similar stages in their lives. These stages can have a great effect on an individual's outlook at any one time. Some of the frustrations and adjustments that come about during any one of them may fade or correct themselves as time goes on.

A mistake many people make at, say 45, is to look for the kind of job that perhaps ten years earlier was their ultimate goal. They don't realize that their needs are different now.

You may have some of the following motivational changes, which are typical in mid-career: (1) You may be anxious to do less of what you're required to do and more of what you want to do. (2) You may not want to do, for say another 20 years, essentially the same thing that you've been doing for the last 10 years or so. (3) You may want to be less involved in details and more with policy making and planning. (4) You undoubtedly are becoming more aware of the need to prepare financially for retirement. (5) You may want the time to develop an activity which you can pursue full-time when you retire.

People in mid-career sometimes fall into the trap of trying to emulate their peers who have been most successful in business. Don't be swayed by how your contemporaries are doing. Regardless of how successful you are, you can always find people to envy for their business success. Your career is a 40-year horse race. Now you are roughly half of the way through it. A few years hence you may pass people who appear to be ahead of you today. The key to your overall career satisfaction is whether you are making reasonable progress toward your long-term life goals and are in a good position to further this progress.

Now let's take a look at how you find an answer to the question, "What do you want to do?" Let's say you are or have been the sales manager of a high technology company. This book aims to help you decide which among several alternatives using a high level of your skills makes the most sense for you—such as management consulting, being a manufacturer's rep in your field of technology, or a position in sales management or marketing. Your skills are like your financial assets. They shouldn't be wasted, unless you are willing to sacrifice them because you feel a strong need to make a major change in your life. This book will not discuss how to change careers. If this is what you want to do, find a counselor who specializes in career changing to help you evaluate possible alternatives. A good place for you to start this process is to read *What Color Is Your Parachute?* by Richard N. Bolles (Berkeley, Calif.: Ten Speed Press, 1980).

**Determining what you want to do**

*Who are you?*

To determine your objectives in your job search and in your life, find out who you are. Start by preparing a summary of the facts of your current situation. Include such things as your job status, age, education, and experience; your financial needs and resources; your strong skills and interests (and deficiencies); work environment preferences; and your family's desired life-style. Establish your primary requirements for a job. Don't make the mistake of undervaluing the factors of work environment and your desired life-style—they can be critical to your job satisfaction in the long run. It's only human to look for a new job that will correct the deficiencies of the old one, and to play down the important things that were right in the latter. Don't get caught in this trap.

Knowing what you can and cannot do is a key ingredient of your career planning. Paul Sargent, for example, is a successful entrepreneur. Over a period of 15 or 20 years he has taken four small, struggling companies (start-ups and failing companies) and straightened them out. Just after he made a switch to a new company several years ago, I asked him, "Why didn't you stay with M&N? It seemed to be going very well." I remember his answer clearly, "Well, I learned something about myself a long time ago," he said. "I have a particular type of expertise, and I also recognize my own limitations. I have found when I get a company up to $5 million or more in sales, it takes a different kind of management than it does when it's smaller. I found that I am much more effective—and really more excited—building up companies when they are small." Here is a man who has been successful and has had a satisfying career—a key to it has been his realistic attitude. Not only does he recognize where his expertise is, but he also recognizes what his limitations are. Furthermore, he has accepted them. Finding out what you can do and recognizing your limitations should be a key part of determining your career requirements.

*Job content*     You'll do best and be happiest over a long period of time in a job that involves your personal interests and values, emphasizes your strengths, and de-emphasizes your weaknesses. You're now at a point where you can broaden or narrow your responsibilities in your field. You also have a chance to seek new challenges. Take this opportunity to ask yourself questions regarding various job alternatives, such as:

1. Are you likely to be happier in a big company or a small one?
2. Are there particular industries that you are

well suited for or that you should avoid? (For example; great opportunity, high risk versus low opportunity, stable organization? Profit versus nonprofit?)

3. Do you prefer to be in a staff or a line role?
4. Would you rather be a specialist in a particular field or would you rather have broader management responsibilities?
5. What kind of people (particularly your boss) would you prefer to work with or should you avoid?
6. How important is the prestige of the company?
7. How important is challenge to you?
8. Are good chances of promotion (including becoming a director) a key factor to you?
9. What kind of management style are you happiest in—loose or highly structured?
10. What sorts of risks are you willing to run?
11. What opportunities will you have after retirement?

You're more likely to be offered a job in a troubled situation—by definition that probably means considerably greater risk. Many persons get in trouble on their jobs, not because of incompetence, but because of circumstances that are beyond their control (i.e., when a company does badly, the standards of performance for the key people are way above normal expectations. Furthermore, in this situation you are much more likely to be faced by a new boss sometime down the road).

*Financial*

Among the important factors in your final choice are the financial ones. They involve making judgments on complex variables: immediate salary versus long-term potential; the degree of risk; potential benefits from incentives, options, etc.; and retirement considerations. At mid-career and beyond, your pension and possibilities for building a nest egg assume more importance as your future working years become limited.

Two factors most influential in the size of a pension are length of service and salary. And in general, higher salaries in the years just before retirement are worth more in accumulating pension credits. If your pension is based on a formula using your last few years' earnings, there is a double incentive to work as long as possible. Also the company's practice concerning when you have to retire may be a high priority for you (although legal requirements are making it more difficult for companies to retire people before age 70).

*Your life-style*

Many people no longer make decisions on a new job largely on the basis of their future careers. Where and how you and your family want to live is also an important consideration. A move from a place that has been happy for your family can exact a price that's far too great to pay for any job. Lots of travel, long hours, and undue pressure also can have a major impact on your family—whether or not you still have any children at home. Another key factor is the opportunity to pursue other interests that may become more important to you as retirement approaches.

Make a list of your job requirements. Then select the eight or ten most important items and put them in priority order.

**Evaluating career alternatives**

Now select the three or four key types of jobs that you would like to consider. There are a number of things you could do with your particular expertise. Most of them will be closely related to what you have done, but don't overlook occupations you have had a yearning for. You may now have the chance of a lifetime to do something quite different. And it might cause a complete change for the better in your career.

You undoubtedly know quite a bit about these career alternatives. You may think you understand them well, and you may. On the other hand, if you have not been in such a role before, you may not appreciate the realities of it. It is particularly important that you do so before you make what may be the most important career decision of your life.

When you talk to people about the reality of working in each of the fields you select, you may find that you don't have as clear an understanding as you thought. Find people on these and related jobs and ask them questions. What are the chances of somebody like myself getting such a position? What is it like on a day-to-day basis? What kind of salary can I expect immediately and in the future? Talk to someone who has been *unsuccessful* in the field. Be realistic about all the negatives (as well as the positives) of each career alternative.

The results of your research may change your views. You may want to revise your list of requirements and their priorities.

Now prepare a table comparing your revised job requirements with each of your career alternatives. This will help you make a logical decision. The table covers much more than what is conventionally thought of as your *job objective.* You will see later how it is summarized for use in your resume and in interviews.

*Conducting your job search*     This process will be described in great detail starting in the next chapter. It covers basically the following activities: preparing your desired-job description, preparing your credentials for your resume and interviews, developing your marketing plan, approaching sources of jobs and contacts to introduce you to possible employers, interviewing, follow-up, negotiating and analyzing offers, and making the final decision.

Your goal should be to get *three offers* that meet a high percentage of your job requirements. If you can select from three good offers you will considerably minimize the risk of a poor choice.

Now let's take a look at a detailed example of how this process is carried out. [The "Career Choice Stages" chart (Table 3-2) shows an overview of Gordon Sampson's job search.] The detailed steps that Sampson took are described in the steps below.

You'll have a pretty good understanding of Gordon Sampson from his "Who Are You?" write-up, which follows:

TABLE 3-2
Career choice stages

Gordon Sampson          Age: 45          Last job: Plant superintendent, 700-employee plant

|  | *Career choice* | | *Job choice* | |
|  | *1* | *2* | *3* | *4* |
|---|---|---|---|---|
| Stage | Evaluation of career alternatives | Decision on most desirable career | Search for job alternatives | Decision on most desirable job offer |
| Procedure | Research on each career (personal interviews and reading) | Evaluation of career alternatives | Job search resulting in offers for specific jobs | Evaluation of specific offers |
| Options | Management consulting Buying a small business Production executive Teaching business and consulting | Production executive | Production manager, ABC Metals Facilities planning manager, Monarch Co. Plant superintendent, Foremost Machine | Facilities planning manager, Monarch Co. |

Gordon Sampson, 73 Bellevue Drive, Glendale, Illinois
Age 45.

Married, 3 children ages 19, 17, 16.

Georgia Tech, AB, 1955, Mechanical Engineering, Honors

Three years as a Tank Corps Officer in the army.

Twenty-one years in production supervision; most recently
Plant Superintendent of a 700-employee machine tool
plant.

Salary $38,000, Bonus $3,500.

No outside income now or in prospect.

Pension accumulation; none (tenure at 3 companies of 9, 8,
and 4 years with no pension vesting).

Present total assets $50,000 (one half earmarked for chil-
dren's college expenses).

Am receiving 3-months severance.

Wife earns $12,000 per year running clothes shop.

| | |
|---|---|
| My strengths: | Excellent knowledge of production pro-cesses. |
| | Prefer planning to line supervision. |
| | Excellent problem solver. |
| | Supervision of technical specialists. |
| My weaknesses: | Weak at company politics. |
| | Don't like confrontation (i.e., dealing with the union). |
| | Detail minded. |
| | Like a controlled environment. |
| Personal: | Have lost job twice (both times company got in trouble). |
| | Wife has spent whole life in area and would be very upset by move—as would children. |
| | Am a homebody—principal interests are family, home, and community (have been active in community). |

All of the items up to "My strengths" are facts,
and were easy for Sampson to record. "My
strengths," "My weaknesses," and to a lesser ex-

tent, "Personal," are subjective items. These subjective items are not always easy to identify.

Sampson's next task was to carefully determine their priority. He did this by using the prioritizing tool illustrated in Table 3-3.

You can determine priorities by your own intuition, but it's not easy to put such a complex set of variables into reasonable order. You will find the prioritizing tool is helpful. Take each important job requirement and test its priority against every other requirement. Focus on each pair of factors, as though they were the only two keys to the decision, and ask yourself which is the more important to you. The matrix used by Sampson will show how this is done by comparing the relative importance of each item to every other item (see Table 3-3).

For example, in thinking of his ideal job, Sampson asked himself, "Is having a low risk job more important to me than its location?" In this case, he decided that location (namely, not moving) which was factor 8, was more important than having a low risk job (i.e., factor 9). Thus, in recording 8 versus 9, 8 (location) is circled. After each factor is evaluated, the number of circles selected for each factor are totaled.

The factor with the highest score is the top priority, the second highest, second, and so on. When there are ties, the higher priority is considered the item of the tie which was the choice over the other. Thus, if location (8) and low risk (9) are tied, the former is considered the higher priority. On the other hand, if 9 was the choice over 8, low risk is considered higher priority. Be careful about having too many factors, for the matrix then becomes unwieldy. Ten factors are probably a practical maximum.

Before you accept the results obtained with this tool, list the priorities in order and see if they

**TABLE 3-3**
Prioritizing job requirements

| | 1. Highest salary | 2. Minimum capital needed | 3. Good long-term prospects | 4. Best chance of getting | 5. Minimum search time | 6. Emphasizes strengths | 7. Deemphasizes weaknesses | 8. Favorable location | 9. Low risk |
|---|---|---|---|---|---|---|---|---|---|
| 1. Highest salary | | | | | | | | | |
| 2. Minimum capital needed | ① 2 | | | | | | | | |
| 3. Good long-term prospects | ① 3 | 2 ③ | | | | | | | |
| 4. Best chance of getting | ① 4 | ② 4 | ③ 4 | | | | | | |
| 5. Minimum search time | ① 5 | ② 5 | 3 ⑤ | 4 ⑤ | | | | | |
| 6. Emphasizes strengths | ① 6 | ② 6 | 3 ⑥ | 4 ⑥ | ⑤ 6 | | | | |
| 7. Deemphasizes weaknesses | ① 7 | ② 7 | 3 ⑦ | 4 ⑦ | ⑤ 7 | 6 7 | | | |
| 8. Favorable location | ① 8 | ② 8 | 3 ⑧ | 4 ⑧ | ⑤ 8 | 6 ⑧ | 7 ⑧ | | |
| 9. Low risk | ① 9 | ② 9 | ③ 9 | 4 ⑨ | ⑤ 9 | ⑥ 9 | ⑦ 9 | ⑧ 9 | |
| Score for each factor | 8 | 2 | 3 | 0 | 7 | 5 | 4 | 6 | 1 |

make sense. You may find that one or two seem to
be rated too high or too low. Examine the answers
given for these items again—your rating may
change. This tool should give you a pretty good
order of your priorities *based on your current
thinking*. When you do your research, and particularly when talking to various employers, you probably will find that your thinking will change. So,
after you have done this research, use the matrix
tool again—you may get a different result.

Sampson's priorities at this stage came out in the
following order.

| *Priority* | *Reasoning* |
|---|---|
| Highest salary | Have maximum need in next six years |
| Minimum search time | Have only three months of severance pay |
| Favorable location | A move would be traumatic for family |
| Emphasizes strengths | Good production knowl-edge; planning rather than line; good technical supervisor; imaginative |
| Deemphasize weaknesses. | Poor salesman and politician; dislike confrontation and crises |
| Good long-term prospects | With my record, they'll take care of themselves |
| Minimum capital needed | Have little available |
| Low risk | Confident that I can always get a good job |
| Best chance of getting | Am optimistic because I have a good record. |

At the start of his campaign Sampson identified
some career alternatives. Let's review his thinking.
Over the years he had worked closely several times
with management consultants. He liked their role
of investigating and making recommendations—two

activities he enjoyed and from which he had derived satisfaction. He preferred this to line supervision. And he liked the variety of things consultants were exposed to—so he thought of consulting as one possibility.

Several good friends had bought their own businesses with limited capital. They had done very well, and Sampson envied them being their own bosses—running their own shows and having comparative freedom. Sampson had been in charge of several large community activities, had achieved good results through his ideas and leadership, and had gotten a lot of satisfaction from them. He felt he had the leadership qualities to operate his own business successfully, if he could find an appropriate one which he could finance reasonably.

About 10 years before, Sampson had been encouraged by someone high-up in educational circles to find a job teaching business courses and consulting on the side. He had given it some thought, but decided at the time he wanted line experience, which a job he had been offered would give him. But since then he had thought about this teaching-consulting type of career occasionally and wondered if he hadn't made a mistake not pursuing it. Sampson liked the idea of an intellectual atmosphere.

Finally, he thought seriously of getting a production-management job such as he had before. This is where he felt his most marketable skills lay.

Any spare time in the first six weeks of Sampson's campaign was spent basically in researching each of these four alternatives. Some was done by reading, but most involved talking with four to six people in each of these fields. He explained to them that he was looking for help and information, and most of them were willing to see him. They also provided him with valuable referrals to other useful people. During this period his resume

included the objective, "Production management,"
which was basically compatible with all the fields
he was exploring.

The following is a list of the principal people
Sampson saw in this research stage:

Four consultants (two large firms, two small
firms).
Two buyers of consulting services.
Two consultants who failed.
Three small-business owners.
Two small-business owners who had failed.
Two venture-capital analysts.
Two bank loan officers.
Two major customers of small businesses.
One supplier of small business.
Three top production executives.
Three professors.
One executive vice president of a business school.

Typical questions Sampson asked were:
What does it take to succeed?
Why do people fail?
What is the earning potential—short term?
What is the earning potential—long term?
Who do you have to satisfy to succeed?
What do they require?
What's involved day-to-day, year-to-year?
What are the greatest risks?
What kind of skills and temperament fit best?

The results of his analysis of the information
Sampson had gathered are shown in Table 3-4.
Prior to the preparation of this matrix, he revised
his priorities, substituting several new ones and
somewhat revising their order. His revised set of
priorities is shown in "My goal" column.

**TABLE 3-4**
Alternative careers analysis, Gordon Sampson

| Job characteristic | My goal | Management consulting | Buy my own business | Production executive | Teaching business-consulting |
|---|---|---|---|---|---|
| Location | Not moving | Won't have to move | Probable move | Probably won't have to move | Probable move |
| Chances of getting | Good | Small with company, could do on my own | Time-consuming; risky | Good; perhaps 500 such jobs within commuting range | Poor; no graduate degree |
| Near term salary | Good salary for six years (children in college) | Minimum for two years; good after five years | Minimum for two years; good after five years | Good immediately | Big decrease until consulting built up (probably three years) |
| Risk | Low | High | High | Moderate | Low |
| Strengths | Good production knowledge; planning rather than line | Selling is critical | Persistence in search; buck stops here; wide variety of skills | Production knowledge; could be planning or supervising | Teaching skill; production knowledge; easier consulting |
| Weaknesses | Poor salesman and politician; dislike confrontation and crises | Feast or famine; lots of competition | Many dream of this; few are successful | Depends on company's success | Building up consulting takes time |
| Capital needs | Have little; small amount from friends | Substantial needed in start-up period | Large amount needed; can finance on possible future increased earnings | None | Some needed in start-up period |
| Long-term prospects | Good salary; good security; pension opportunity | If successful, good; can continue forever | If successful, good; can continue forever | Depends on company's success; probably steady salary increases; reasonable pension; fixed retirement date | Fair remuneration; a good life; can continue consulting after retirement |

Note: Several lesser priorities were shown on a second page (which is not included here).

Essentially the changes in priorities were that top salary and minimum search time were not critical, as long as they were reasonable. Furthermore, the chance of getting the job he wanted and the job being relatively low risk moved from low to near the top of his priorities.

From his research Sampson concluded that management consulting was unrealistic. Success in consulting depends primarily on something he was weak in; namely, selling. Furthermore, he needed a good income immediately for his family's education, and a consulting business would, at best, take several years to build up. Finally, he was temperamentally unsuited to the traveling and the ups-and-downs and pressures of consulting.

As for buying his own business, it soon became obvious that this was also a pipe dream, basically for similar reasons. Sampson needed immediate income, and it would have been sheer folly to risk his limited capital. In addition, searching for a sound and suitable business to buy would undoubtedly be time-consuming.

The teaching-consulting alternative was temperamentally suited to Sampson. On the other hand, such jobs were few in number, and he would have to accept an immediate substantial drop in income. Consulting income would supplement his salary in time. But this would take several years because as a new faculty member his top priority would be establishing his reputation in the classroom.

A production executive's job similar to his former one made the most sense. In the first place, there were a number of them available. Within his commuting range, he estimated there were perhaps 500 such jobs. With normal turnover, probably several of them were open at any one time, and by this time he had had interviews for three. Furthermore, there was the possibility of additional such jobs being established if he could get companies to recognize a critical need his experience could meet. Already an interesting position of this kind had come to his attention. There was a lot of variety in these jobs—so by being selective he felt he could find one tailored to his particular combination of skills, interests (and weaknesses). Sampson decided to make his objective a production executive's job.

Note the insight Sampson obtained through this research process. First, he gained a much better understanding of what his real requirements were. Second, in taking time to explore several career alternatives, Sampson got a much better understanding of their requirements. So he reduced his chance of accepting an unsuitable job. This process also put these alternatives into proper focus for the future. Should difficult times arise on the new job, it would be unlikely that he would wish that he had chosen one of the other alternatives. Gordon Sampson was not stupid. But he was going through a period of great uncertainty in his life with an important and emotional decision to make.

When he started out, Sampson found it easy to delude himself into thinking of himself as he wanted to be, not as what he was. However, as he talked with people, he got a better idea of what really made him tick—his strengths, his weaknesses, his interests, his values, and their priorities. It would have been difficult for anyone else to convince Sampson of the right answer—he had to find it himself. *Your best guarantee of making a sound decision is to go through the tedious hard work Sampson did.* Your background and needs are different—so your job characteristics and priorities will be different, but you can use Sampson's example as a guide. If pursued aggressively, this process can be accomplished in a month.

In evaluating alternate choices (such as career alternatives) it is often helpful to put a value on each of the priorities and then to rate each factor for each alternative. For example, "Chance of getting" might be 20 percent, with "Production executive" being given a rating of 16 percent and "Teaching business-consulting" 5 percent. Then a cumulative score for each alternative can be tallied for comparison. Be careful not to put undue emphasis on this refinement. For example, an alternative with a total value of 82 is clearly more in line with your priorities than one with 67, but it probably has about the same rating for you as one with 80.

Having made the decision on his job goal, Sampson polished up his resume and specifically targeted it to a production executive's job. He then started an intensive marketing campaign for such a job. Having improved his skills in getting in to see people and conducting interviews, he found his batting average increased. Several of the people he saw in his career-alternative phase were helpful again. As a middle-aged executive it took time to develop a number of high-quality job alternatives—but they did come! Finally, he had three good offers.

To evaluate the offers, Sampson used a process which was similar to that for evaluating his alternative-career possibilities. First, he rated the key considerations by using the matrix. Of course several of the factors considered in evaluating career alternatives were no longer valid: length of search, chances of getting, and capital needed. However, various new factors became important. "Why was the job available?" became important in rating the organizational dynamics of the job. Other new factors were: the company's reputation, the base to move from (if the job failed), pressure, traveling, the type of people, and prestige.

Salary assumed much less importance at this stage because all three offers were about the same. A much more important aspect of salary was the likelihood of it being available over a long period of time (i.e., the risk factor). The "Alternative Jobs Analysis" chart (Table 3-5) shows Sampson's assessment of the principal factors.

Sampson's evaluation of the three offers was:

1. Production manager, ABC Metals—he had serious reservations about the company's future, its reputation for handling people, his negative reaction to several of the people there, and the way that the job had been structured. By this time he had become aware of the fact that sometimes an employer sets up a job without carefully structuring it. The person hired to fill it fails because of the lack of the employer's foresight. Unfortunately, the person hired is the biggest loser.

2. Facilities planning manager, Monarch Co.—his overall reaction to the company, the type of requirements of the job, its people, and its long-term future was positive. He had serious questions about becoming a superspecialist in a limited field (one he was not intimately familiar with, but which he felt he could handle well). However, he felt this was offset by the excellent reputation of the company. He was disappointed in the salary—it was the lowest of the three alternatives—but he felt this would be offset in time by the company's more certain growth prospects. The job involved more traveling than he wanted, but this was a drawback he felt he could live with.

3. Plant superintendent, Foremost Machine—he liked the company, its type of business (very similar to his last company), and its overall reputation. On the minus side, he had the feeling the company was a prime candidate for a merger. In addition, his would be a line job, he'd have to deal with a tough union, and he sensed a lack of professionalism in management.

In the course of his search, Sampson ran into two people who he felt stood out as being sup-

**TABLE 3-5**
Alternative jobs analysis, Gordon Sampson

| Job characteristics | My goal | Production manager ABC Metals | Facilities planning manager–Monarch Co. | Plant superintendent Foremost Machine |
|---|---|---|---|---|
| Type of company | – | 1,800 employees, 1 plant, metal fabrication | 15,000 employees, 17 plants, electronics | 1,000 employees, 1 plant, metal fabrication |
| Job duties | Planning—not line | Overseeing 27 employee department—report to plant superintendent | Overseeing design and construction of all plants; report to manufacturing vice president; supervise 12 | Overseeing all production; 700 employees; report to manufacturing vice president |
| Location | Don't want to move | No immediate move, possibly one later | No immediate move nor likely in long run | No immediate move nor likely in long run |
| Risk | Low | Moderate | Low | Moderate |
| Near-term salary | $50,000 minimum | $50,000 + 5% to 10% bonus | $47,500 + 10% bonus | $51,000 + 5% to 10% bonus |
| Why available? | – | New position—formerly part of plant superintendent's duties | Sudden death of predecessor | Current superintendent retiring |
| Type of people | Prefer high grade professionals | Known as tough people; didn't like two of five I met (including prospective boss) | Excellent reputation; liked everyone I met, especially prospective boss | Liked everyone, though several didn't seem very professional |
| Strengths | Good production knowledge, planning rather than line; good technical supervisor | Planning job; suitable supervisory role | Planning job; suitable supervisory role | Line job; difficult supervisory role |

| | | | | |
|---|---|---|---|---|
| Weaknesses | Poor salesman and politician; dislike confrontation and crises | Superintendent does not want to give up role | Limited similar experience (though capable of doing job) | Difficult union situation |
| Long-term prospects | Good salary, good security, good pension | Long term, but erratic growth; good chance to be superintendent when he retires in four years | Long term stable growth; little chance of promotion | Fair; strong family control; merger candidate; good chance to be manufacturing vice president in seven years |
| Base to move from | Strong base | Good—universally needed experience | Limited; would be super-specialist in a large company | Good; universally needed experience |
| Company's reputation | Good | Fair; several large layoffs in ten years; lots of turnover; poor place to work | Excellent; no real layoffs; low turnover; good place to work | Good; seems way behind times; moderate layoffs and turnover; fair place to work |
| Traveling | Don't want over 10% | Practically none | About one fifth of time | Practically none |
| Pressure | Moderate | High | Moderate | High |
| Prestige | Of moderate importance | Low | High | Good |

portive and who had impressed him with their common sense. He arranged a meeting with each of them, and with a close friend whose judgment he particularly respected. With each he reviewed in some depth the pros and cons of each job offer. While he came away with some unresolved questions, his judgment was confirmed: he should accept the offer as facilities planning manager of Monarch Co. Seven years later this decision turned out to be a wise one. The job has gone very well—the company has progressed nicely, his job has expanded in scope, and he likes the people he works with.

Once again, notice the further refinement of Sampson's requirements, caused by his exposure to several job possibilities. Location, job duties, risk, and the kind of people he'd be working with moved up in priority, while salary became less important.

Incidentally, many of his friends thought that Sampson could have gotten a "better" job than he did. In fact, two of his closest and most successful friends strongly recommended that he take a job with a start-up, high-technology company and "make a lot of money." Sampson knew, however, the high risk of these companies and the tremendous turnover in personnel. He realized such a job wasn't for him. This is a concrete example of the need to evaluate all advice regardless of who gives it.

One final thought. Sampson is reasonably sure he wouldn't have made the decision he did if the Monarch Metal job had been offered to him in the first month. At that time he was thinking primarily of management consulting, buying his own business, or being a plant superintendent or manufacturing vice president. The time taken to make his final decision in an orderly and careful manner was time well spent—and probably necessary for Sampson to take, not just to find a job, but to find a really suitable one.

**Some summary thoughts**

1. If at the start of this process, you can't narrow your career alternatives to two to four choices, consult a vocational counselor. College placement offices, executive recruiters, and employment agencies can usually recommend such a service.

2. Your success in one company won't necessarily be transferred to success in another. Your important achievements may have been only partly due to your ability. They may have been as much due to the needs of your former company at the time and the chemistry surrounding your role in the organization. A prospective company may *appear* to have the need for many of these same skills, but the management may not really understand what it's going to take to let you get similar results. If this is the case and you accept such a job, you'll be the real loser.

3. You'll find a change in career usually takes longer to achieve than another job in your last field. Often a career change means lower pay. It also means greater risk, because its success involves a much greater number of unknowns. If this is your choice—and it has been successful for many—make sure you research it thoroughly. Bear in mind people in the prospective field may try to dissuade you because you don't have the background. Make sure you convince yourself that this is valid before giving up. If you explore the background of many in the field, you'll likely find quite a few came to it with quite different types of experience.

4. If you're like most people in the "Advanced development" phase of a career or beyond (Table 3-1), you're determined that this change be your last. That's natural. Realize, however, your needs—

financial, job interest, and satisfaction—are likely to change. What may seem like the right job for you now may well be so structured that it doesn't leave much flexibility. What you may have to do then is what many people do (particularly when they're well along in their careers): spend more time on other aspects of life—friends, hobbies, community activities, travel, and so on.

5. Much has been written about the mid-life crisis. Articles in the popular press are frequent, calling attention to dramatic examples of people making major changes in their lives in their 40s and 50s. These instances do happen, but they tend to be blown out of proportion. On the other hand, changes in aspects of your life are occurring and affecting your attitudes and aspirations. As mentioned earlier, you may or may not have realized you're never going to achieve your ultimate career goal. Or if you do, you may not get the satisfaction you expected. Your life-style may well have changed or be changing. Your children may have moved away, and you may have more demanding family responsibilities with aging relatives. Or you may be divorced or separated. You may feel you're losing your motivation. Believe me, it's still there— but what triggers it may be less job oriented and more influenced by other parts of your life—civic affairs, continuing education, whatever—or even different aspects of the job. If you take time to get these things in focus, you will find you have built a strong base for the rest of your life.

6. Don't try to emulate others—you'll likely end up making a decision that isn't right for you. The pattern of success for many varies over the years and should be measured by a lot more than the job you hold. Many of the people most successful in their careers have paid a high price in their personal lives.

7. If you have a strong inclination toward an overcrowded field (e.g., teaching), research it carefully—you may find it isn't as crowded as you think.

Having determined your job goal, let's next examine what employers look for in candidates.

# Chapter four

# WHAT EMPLOYERS ARE LOOKING FOR

**Employers have problems too**

Ask most job hunters how their campaign is going and they will reply, "Good jobs are hard to find." Ask most employers how their hiring is going, and they will reply, "Good people are hard to find." A surprisingly high percentage of jobs advertised in *The Wall Street Journal* and *New York Times* are still unfilled three months after the ads run. This isn't because there are no qualified candidates. Sorting out the candidates, evaluating the best, getting agreement on selection, and negotiating terms of employment can be a complex and slow process —and good people are hard to find.

**A difficult recruitment**

The controller of XYZ, Betty Black, was responsible for installing her company's first computer. Within a short time, the computer operation was in trouble—costs were too high, there were many errors, and much of the work was behind schedule. She and her computer manager disagreed on corrective action. The manager wanted to expand the computer's workload and bring in new equipment. Black wanted to get their current system under control. After a year of this controversy, Black fired the computer manager and started looking for a replacement.

After six weeks of aggressive recruiting, Black's personnel manager (a good recruiter) had referred only two candidates to her, and they were both poor ones.

One day Black stormed into the personnel manager's office. In addition to an already busy workload, she was getting many of the computer problems dumped in her lap. Black was ready to hire almost anyone. The personnel manager showed Black a file of more than 100 resumes of candidates for the job. At the personnel manager's urging, Black decided to take them home to select candidates she wanted to interview. As she was leaving, the personnel manager predicted, "I'll bet you'll be back in here tomorrow morning and tell me you don't want to interview any of them." Sure enough, the prediction was exactly on target.

Years later, in retrospect, Black observed that probably 30 percent of these candidates were technically qualified. However, the best candidates' resumes all emphasized accomplishments in expanding installations and upgrading equipment. Little, if any, emphasis was put on improving the day-to-day management of the department. Because of her previous experience, Black had a bias against this type of candidate. She saw that these applicants had the same approach to the job as her former computer manager. Black's view as controller was not unique. She belonged to two trade associations of senior financial executives. When the subject of computers came up at meetings, they all expressed widespread dissatisfaction with the mismanagement of their data-processing installations.

A key to being an effective job hunter is to understand the major things that employers are likely to be looking for in your field of expertise. One of your liabilities may be the narrowness of your view concerning the variety of jobs in your field and their requirements. Your view is probably colored by your experience with your former organization and by your former boss's view of the job. This narrowness of outlook may be well fixed if you have worked in the same company for a long time. It may prompt you to overlook suitable job opportunities, or to block yourself out by targeting your resume to jobs similar to your old one. So you should design your resume to show a wide range of skills in your field. Later you will see how your credentials should be organized to appear most favorably in relation to the specific type of job you're seeking.

**Recruitment difficulties happen frequently**

Employers have recruitment problems because they demand high standards and the hiring process is complicated. Develop the ability to look at yourself as a candidate in the same way an employer would. To do this, try to recall some of the recruitments you have made in the past. Why did certain candidates impress you? Why did others fail? Undoubtedly part of this failure was due to problems in your own recruitment practices, for example, unrealistic or vague specifications, ineffective sources of people, and so on. But part of it was due to the ineffective ways that candidates presented themselves. Were they completely self-oriented? Were they adequately prepared? Were some way off target in presenting their experience relative to your needs? Answers to these questions can be helpful in your preparation and interviews.

When it comes to a final candidate selection, an employer makes a judgment on three bases:

1. Does the job hunter have strong (not always the best) technical qualifications compared to other candidates?

2.  Is the individual likely to fit in with the basic style of the boss and the organization ("Is he or she our kind of person?")?
3.  Does the applicant have the motivation to solve the job's most important problems?

**Your job description**

Present yourself as the person who is as close as possible to what an employer is likely to be looking for. Start out by asking yourself what skills and personal characteristics you would want to hire if you were the manager trying to fill this position.

Do you really know or do you just think you know? Not long ago, a senior executive recruiter from one of the country's largest firms stated that she recently conducted three searches for chief financial officers—and the fundamental requirement for each was quite different. One was for an individual strong in financial control systems, one for a merger-and-acquisition specialist, and one for a capital-raising specialist. A good resume for a chief financial officer should include, if possible, accomplishments in all three of these functions, among other things. *Make sure your accomplishments show the widest range in the functions of your job objective.*

To get better perspective on the market for your skills, one of the first steps is to write a *realistic* description of the job you're seeking. A general job description of the type found in most manuals is not good enough. You will need one that outlines the key functions of the job in depth (the important items that are critical in an employer's decision to hire).

The job description should be an expansion of the survey described in Chapter 3, What Do You Want to Do? Make a list of the principal functions and personal attributes shown in *The Wall Street Journal* and *New York Times* ads for similar jobs and tally their frequency. Then prepare a job description listing the functions and personal characteristics required in order of importance. In resumes, in letters, and in interviews try to appear as close to the *ideal candidate* as possible. Don't worry if you're quite far from it, because almost everybody else will be too. The closer you can appear to the ideal candidate, the more favorable an impression you're likely to make.

This exercise is important because it will help identify functional experience you lack. Part of your preparation will be to develop a strategy to cope with this. It can be done by showing that you have had comparable experience, you have frequently handled new challenges well, and that you are a fast learner.

Another slant on understanding an employer's point of view is to ask yourself, "What are the main reasons sales managers (or whatever) fail on the job?" Some of these reasons will be paramount in the minds of prospective employers. Obviously many don't meet their company's sales goals. The same with expense targets and the various other functions listed above. In addition, though, there are many other things which are required for success on the job—developing imaginative plans, being sensitive to the boss's quirks, preparing timely and accurate reports, and so on. Make a list of as many of these as you can.

**The importance of personal characteristics**

The conventional approach to preparing your credentials is stressing technological skills. These are extremely important—you need a high level of skills for the job you're seeking. However, often the choice between top candidates for an executive job is based on personal characteristics. Betty Black was turned off by qualified computer-manager candidates because of their apparent bias on the requirements of the job. As you will see in the chapter on improving interviewing effectiveness, the key is to find out early the requirements the employer feels are needed most in the person to be hired. You can and should predict pretty well what the employer's likely top priorities are for such a job.

Many of these nontechnical attributes are applicable to any job—and should be developed in your preparation. These are such things as:

Do you consistently do good work?

Do you get jobs done on time? Within budget?

Are you resourceful (i.e., will you find a solution to critical problems where others won't)?

Do you anticipate problems—rather than react to them?

Do you keep your boss well informed?

Are you 100 percent loyal?

Are you a team player?

Do you get along well with people at all levels?

Do you follow through?

Is your first priority to help your boss get done what he or she needs to get done?

Do you get the nitty-gritty done (often a key to success on a job) as well as perform well on the major projects?

Do you set priorities and work toward them?

Are you effective in developing people?

Do you have good credibility?

Are you somebody who is well informed and continually learning?

Do you follow company policy?

Are you known for being thorough?

Do you work well under pressure?

From your lists of skills and personal attributes, developed from ads, and your list of the reasons why executives fail in your type of job, develop a list of the job requirements.

Select 12 to 15 of the most important and arrange them in priority order. These are the items
that should be emphasized in your resume and in
personal interviews. Such a list is shown in the
accompanying sample job description for a sales
manager.

Job description—Sales manager

Education: College degree, preferably in business and
economics.

Experience: 15-20 years in sales and sales management.

Personal characteristics: Persuasive, aggressive, flexible, outgoing, innovative, and competitive.

Working conditions: High pressure, constantly working under hard-to-make and easy-to-measure targets, lots of travel, lots of entertaining, and long
hours.

Long-range possibilities: Good opportunity to move
into top management (often to vice president of
sales if you develop administrative skills).

Pros: Challenging, exciting, high compensation
(based more on your success than in most fields),
great opportunity to make your mark.

Cons: Continual pressure, very demanding on personal life, high risk.

Functional experience needed (in decreasing order of
importance):

Increasing sales.

Decreasing expenses.

Improving profit margins.

Building an effective sales force.

Introducing new products.

Developing new markets.

Improving distribution methods.

Reducing field inventory.

Now that you have identified the key things an employer may be looking for in the job you're seeking, examine your experience, aiming to present it most effectively.

# Chapter five

# WHAT DO YOU HAVE TO OFFER?

**"I really don't have many accomplishments"**

Bill Jackson was an experienced executive in his late 40s. He lost his job as assistant chief engineer of Maverick Ltd. when his boss retired and a new engineering vice president was brought in. Although Bill had been job hunting for several months, he had not had an offer that really interested him.

One day Bill had a particularly discouraging interview with Champion Company—it was for a job which really excited him and for which he felt well qualified. But he was sure that he had failed in the interview. That evening as he was getting his thoughts together for an interview with Arrow Company the next day, his mind wandered back to the experience at Champion. As he thought about it, he suddenly became indignant and blurted out, "I know damn well I'm qualified for that Champion job. After all, I straightened out the development-engineering problems on the Widget Project which everyone else was ready to give up on—and it went on to become one of Maverick's most profitable lines. Then I reengineered the What's Its line when it was going down hill so drastically, and it became reestablished as one of the most important products of the company."

Bill went on to recall three similar accomplishments. He realized that he had never even mentioned two of the items in his resume or in any of the seven or eight interviews he had had to date. He also realized that he had mentioned two other accomplishments only briefly in a couple of interviews because he assumed that the employers would automatically understand the full implications of them. Judging from their reaction, they apparently didn't.

For example, Bill had completely overlooked one activity: his membership on the building committee for a major addition to his church. This gave him valuable experience in dealing with an architect and in overseeing construction. Aspects of this experience, including his persuading the committee to select a relatively unknown architect—which turned out to be a very successful choice—were important points in his being offered his next job as a division general manager. Overlooking key accomplishments is frequently a way job hunters undersell themselves.

In every first interview Bill had had, he had been asked to describe his education. In each case he explained that he had been to the University of Kentucky and had majored in mechanical engineering. In reviewing the Champion interview, he recognized that he had been greatly understating the implications of this education.

So, in the Arrow interview the next day Bill described it in this way, "I went to the University of Kentucky and majored in mechanical engineering. While I was there I carried on a 20-hour-a-week job which allowed me to pay 75 percent of my expenses. I graduated with honors with a B+ average and at the same time was able to play three years on the baseball team and was vice president of my fraternity." The executive vice president of Arrow was obviously impressed and he stated, "That shows that you are obviously damn smart and highly motivated." This example illustrates another great difficulty for many job hunters—they communicate their accomplishments ineffectively. Bill Jackson's experience is not unusual at all according to many of the best outplacement consultants. In fact, less than 1 percent of all job hunters overstate their accomplishments, and the vast majority greatly understate them. Let's see now how you can overcome this difficulty.

**Recognizing your major accomplish- ments**

A key to selling yourself is to show examples of what you've done—your accomplishments. To get a complete list of your accomplishments, you may have to tap your subconscious—which you can easily do by following the steps listed in the next couple of pages. Your first step is to make a comprehensive list of them. For each of your jobs list all of your responsibilities and your key accomplishments in them—include even the minor ones. See "Your Job Accomplishments Chart" (Table 5-1). To help you recall your accomplishments, think about the changes that had a considerable effect on your job. For example:

A new boss.

A sale or a merger of the company.

A new system.

A new subordinate.

New equipment (such as a computer).

A new peer you worked closely with.

A new product.

New legislation.

A new office or plant.

**TABLE 5-1**
Your job accomplishments chart

| Dates | Company | Title | Responsibility | Accomplishments |
|---|---|---|---|---|
| 7/73-11/75 | MNO | Buyer | Reducing purchase prices | Change of competitive bidding system<br>Concentration on large volume items<br>Maxim castings |
| | | | Coping with short supply | Rescheduling Magna stainless steel |
| | | | Developing new sources | General Rubber<br>Foxcroft housings |
| | | | Etc. | |
| 11/75 | Peerless Machinery | Assistant purchasing agent | Administration | Reorganization plan<br>Emphasis on use of typing pool<br>Weekly meetings of buyers |
| | | | Subcontracting | Revised program<br>Developed new contract |
| | | | Improved reporting | Computerization<br>Daily shortage report<br>Weekly variation from plan |
| | | | Etc. | |

These *peg points* provide an easy method of recall-
ing various things you did on a job that you may
have forgotten. For each peg point, ask yourself
what changes occurred in your work and what
were your resulting accomplishments. For example, four years ago Jane Foster came in as purchasing agent. Several months afterward Bill Smith was
moved over from buyer of raw materials to buyer
of subcontract assemblies. A few months later
Smith was asked to be department coordinator on
the new quality-control system. Foster's appointment was a peg point for Smith to recall these two
changes in his duties.

Another useful way to analyze your experience
is to write down your answers to the following
questions.

What promotions have you been given? Why
were you promoted?

What merit salary increases have you been given?
What were the comments of your boss when he
gave you these increases?

What added responsibilities were you given in
any of your jobs? What comments were made
as these assignments were given to you?

What committee assignments have you been
given in addition to the regular responsibilities
of your job?

What other leadership roles have you assumed
on the job or in the community?

What special projects were you given in addition
to the regular functions of your job?

Under what circumstances were you asked to
represent your organization to outsiders (either
on the company premises or outside)?

Where have you excelled over your peers in any
activity?

Your files also can be another useful memory jogger, as can your diary or expense books. The buddy system of working with another job hunter in a brainstorming session can often help you recall past achievements you might otherwise overlook.

After completing your list of job accomplishments make a list, starting in college, of all of the major nonjob activities you can think of (community work, major hobbies, extracurricular college activities) to identify accomplishments in them.

In this set of exercises, undoubtedly there will be duplications. Don't worry about that. Just make the *most exhaustive list* of your accomplishments that you can. Don't shortchange yourself on these exercises, because they can be the most important aspect of your campaign preparation. You probably won't be able to think of everything at one sitting so keep a notebook handy in case any more ideas crop up. This is the time to "toot your own horn."

Now select those accomplishments which are *most marketable for the job you are seeking.* Select 12 to 15, using your job description as a reference point (see Chapter Four, "Your Job Description"). Also select any others that might have some marketability in interviews. These worksheets may be useful for future reference.

You may have realized that you are missing a key item of functional experience although you are well qualified in other aspects. Coping with this deficiency is explained in Chapter Fourteen.

Different stages in a project can mean different accomplishments or skills. For example, you may have been responsible for the computerization of a system in your department. You may have had major involvement in various stages such as the analysis of the old system, the development of the new one, the implementation phase, the use of the resulting system, and expansion or refinement of it at a later time. Each phase may represent somewhat different skills and accomplishments.

A single accomplishment may offer an opportunity to demonstrate a number of key skills and personal characteristics. For example, you may have prepared a report that brought about an important change in the company's operating procedures, a change that met with considerable resistance. Such a report could show your skills in being analytical, persuasive, having perseverance, being imaginative, working under pressure, ability to meet a deadline, and so on.

**Presenting your accomplishments**

How can you present these accomplishments most effectively? To help there is an easy formula called PAR—P = Problem, A = Action, R = Result. For each of your key accomplishments answer: What was the problem? What action did you take? What was the result? You will find it worthwhile to take the time to outline each one of your PARs in writing. You will use them many times in your campaign.

Exhibit 5-1 is an example of the PAR formula. Sometimes important experiences don't lend themselves to it easily. Exhibit 5-2 is a write-up of such an experience. Note that not only does such a write-up show how to outline your accomplishments in detail to make a satisfactory presentation in your interviews, but it also serves as an example of a condensation of each, suitable for your resume. Underline key words and phrases to identify the highlights you want to include in your resume. Spend considerable time on the wording of each of your accomplishments for your resume. You will find numerous examples of good wording in the resumes in Chapter Six. Note the importance of using action words. A key point to get across is

EXHIBIT 5-1
A PAR write-up

---

Problem: *Company's field selling expenses were too high.* It had 157 high-overhead company-operated branches for large sales volume areas. Also it used 107 independent, low-cost distributors for low-volume areas.

Action: A spot check showed several branches didn't have the sales volume to carry the overhead and a number of distributorships had more than enough volume to be branches. *Developed a computer analysis* for measuring the key variables: sales volume, sales potential, the profitability of mix, and expenses. *Also* developed a formula for determining breakeven between branch and distributor operations. *Helped put together a program* to implement changes revealed by this analysis, including setting of sales and expense budgets.

Result: In three months field selling expenses for $25,000,000 company decreased $187,000 on annual basis. By the end of the year, the profit improvement was at the rate of $284,000 annually.

---

*Summary for your resume*

Was a key member of a team carrying out a sales-expense reduction program saving almost $200,000 annually. Developed computer analysis which provided basic data for program.

**EXHIBIT 5-2**
A typical experience write-up (of a junior staff assistant)

Represented firm at national meetings

Traveled to Chicago, Houston, New York, Washington, etc., as company's representative at national security analysts meetings. Others attending were vice presidents and other high officials of many of the top investment firms.

Took extensive notes on the formal presentations. Took part in the discussions. Asked questions to get information needed for our firm. Made contacts for our firm. At Chicago meeting met John Jones who became a customer.

Interpreted data presented and summarized in a report, interpreting most important points. Made recommendations for action.

My reports were circulated to the chairman of the board, president, and other senior officials of the firm. On several occasions these reports were favorably commented on by them.

*Summary for your resume*

Participated for my firm at economic and investment meetings in various parts of the country with top officials of many of the best known national investment firms. Reported the results with recommendations to top management.

how effectively you work out solutions to problems and work with people in getting them implemented.

Examining your accomplishments in depth will provide you with the basic information you need for your resume. Now let's see how to put this material together to put your best foot forward.

# Chapter six

# A RESUME TO PUT YOUR BEST FOOT FORWARD

**Do you
need one?**

Yes.

Some job hunters have succeeded without resumes because they were able to present themselves effectively in another way—by writing an impressive personal letter, getting interviews through telephone cold calls, and so on. Some job counselors agree that a resume is unnecessary, at least initially. They say you can always submit one after the interview, and tailor it to the particular job.

My advice is: consider yourself typical. A strong resume emphasizing your objective and background, *properly composed and used,* is your most effective job-hunting tool. And most job counselors agree. Not only is it useful for getting the proper entrées, but it forces you to organize what you have to sell. This makes it easier to be effective in interviews.

Unfortunately, many people have poor experience with resumes because they don't know how to prepare and present them. Resume or no, all counselors agree, the most critical mistake that many job hunters make is failing to analyze what they have to offer and developing an effective means of presenting it.

**Does a good resume make a difference?**

Paul Johnson was a production executive with 20 years' experience who lost his job in a merger. During several months of his job search he relied primarily on a network of personal contacts, with little success. He finally decided to mail his resume to a large number of companies. Recognizing the importance of this mailing, Johnson carefully revised his resume. He then asked four people he knew who were interested in helping job hunters to evaluate it.

Johnson was delighted when these four people, after careful thought, told him that his resume was essentially a good one and that only superficial changes were needed. Johnson then mailed his letter and new resume to 100 company presidents and asked for an interview. And after three weeks, he had not received one response.

Shortly afterward, Johnson ran into a friend who had just been through a job search. This successful job hunter said she'd be happy to go over the document, and the first thing she said when Johnson met with her was, "Your resume is no good." In an hour she helped him revise it. Johnson mailed this revision to 250 presidents—and got 21 interviews and four good job offers.

What was the difference between the first and second resumes? Johnson's first was probably fairly typical. The second differed in two important ways: (1) In the second resume, Johnson's accomplishments were much more clear and dramatically worded, and (2) the accomplishments selected were those that were more likely to appeal to an employer who was trying to fill the kind of job Johnson was looking for.

**A good resume is a good ad**

The typical resume is a simple chronological listing of background and experience. This makes it easy for recruiters or employers to categorize an applicant. But any competent job counselor will tell you that this isn't enough. Your resume should be *your personal advertisement for a job*. The word *advertisement* is chosen because your resume should clearly organize your experience to create the most favorable impression for you (both initially and after careful reading). A simple listing will not do this.

What does a good ad do? It attracts attention and it makes it easy for the reader to get the message. It's oriented to the reader, it highlights favorable points, it's easy to read, and the details stand out under careful reading. What does a good ad avoid? It doesn't try to get the whole message across, and it doesn't include (or at least plays down) negative points. A good resume should adhere to the same standards.

**The employer's point of view**

Employers are deluged with resumes. Your goal is to get your resume into the hands of *executives who can hire you and to make sure it is given careful consideration.* To accomplish this goal, it must answer the questions that almost always run through an employer's mind when reading a resume. What kind of a job is this person looking for? This triggers two other questions: (1) Do I have any real need for a person in this field of expertise? (2) Is this person worth the time of an interview? Your resume has to make clear the kind of a job you're looking for and make a convincing case that you have strong credentials for such a position. Most people read a newspaper story in the following manner: first, the headline; then if they're interested, the lead paragraph; and finally, if their interest continues, the whole story. A great many people read a resume in the same way: first to get a general impression, next to look for details necessary to support a decision on whether to grant an interview. Your resume must make a strong initial impression but it also has to stand up under careful reading.

Professional recruiters have the most demanding standards for evaluating resumes. They are skilled in evaluating applicants for positions that have been carefully defined by others. Within perhaps 30 seconds these professionals decide on which pile a resume goes: "probably interested," "possibly interested," or "not interested." The "probably interested" will definitely be given more careful screening. The "possibly interested" may. The "not interested" (usually 90 percent or more) definitely won't. Recruiters first look for people whose qualifications match the job specs closely. After several interviews and a careful check of references, these professionals then select for referral to the employer those candidates whose qualifications and personal chemistry seem to fit best.

Most executives read resumes only occasionally, and they are more flexible in their appraisal of them. They put a high priority on personal compatibility. They want key people on their team that they relate to well, so a close match to the job specs is of lesser importance. These executives also have considerable latitude to create jobs for people they want on their team. A resume that scores well with professional recruiters should score equally well with operating executives. The converse is not true. A good unconventional resume may be of little interest to a professional recruiter, but it may catch and hold a key executive's attention.

Employers look for specialists. They seek them out, offer them the highest salaries, and give them the most challenging jobs. Big company recruiters try to recruit specialists or potential specialists on college campuses. Executive recruiters find their specialists in major jobs in business and industry. If you're seeking a job with a large- or medium-sized company you should present yourself in such a specialist role. Except in small companies, the job market is poor for the jack-of-all-trades. The most successful professional job counselors urge you to set a specific objective and mold all your presentations to it.

Maybe you think that you should present yourself as a generalist because it makes you a candidate for a wide variety of jobs. While in theory this broadens your market, by using such a straddling approach you won't appear as a strong candidate for any job. But if you show good credentials for a job that's not available, you may be offered another job in the company.

**A chronological or a functional resume?**

Almost all resumes fit into one of two classifications: chronological or functional, although there are some that are basically a combination of the two. William S. Morrison's (see Resume 6-1) is the most common type—chronological. This shows experience in reverse chronological order, starting with the most recent job. The resume of Frank J. Harrison (Resume 6-2) is functional. Here the prime emphasis is on type of experience (regardless of when and where it occurred). A purely functional resume would not include the employment section on the second page. Leaving this section out would reduce the resume's effectiveness for an executive. Including it where it is, however, puts the emphasis on the type of experience the individual has and plays down where and when it was accumulated.

Most professional recruiters prefer a chronological resume because an employment record is easy to understand. Recruiting personnel evaluate you primarily on your record of job progress and increasing accomplishments. If you have a good record of advancement in a single field, a chronological resume is probably best for you. A chrono-

RESUME 6-1
Chronological resume of a sales manager with an excellent record

This record shows how he steadily acquired increasing responsibilities and discharged them with increasing success. A strong candidate for executive recruiters.

---

William S. Morrison                              Married
37 Grove Street                                  2 children
Fort Wayne, Indiana  56923                       Excellent health
405-738-9563


Job
Objective:  A.* Senior Marketing Executive

          B.  MUNSON PUMPS COMPANY, Fort Wayne, Indiana
              Manufacturers of pumps for paper and chemical industries.
              Sales $37,000,000.

          C.  Sales Manager (1976-     )
              Responsible for sales force of 147 salesmen and 69 distributors in 32 states.

          D.  Increased sales 32% from $28,000,000 in 1976. Reduced
              seven regional warehouses to five at an annual savings of
              $260,000.

              Reorganized sales force so sales volume done by distributors 27% now was 21% four years ago. Annual savings
              $190,000.

              Turnover reduced from 37% per year to 23%.

              Through improved selection, training, and sales support
              have increased sales per man 31%.

              By increased emphasis on high profit lines and revised
              pricing policies, increased gross profits from 31% to 35%.

              Assistant to Vice President of Sales (1970-1976)
              Coordinated development and introduction to market of
              new lines of pumps with more than double the capacity of
              any produced before. Currently they are almost 20% of
              company sales volume and most profitable of all product
              lines.

RESUME 6-1 *(continued)*

Developed computer analysis of profitability of 39 company branches and 58 distributors. Set product line sales targets for each based on market potential. Also set expense goals.

When company acquired Ventor Hydraulics, developed and carried out plan for consolidation of two sales organizations which minimized turnover and confusion.

Originated design modifications of XL line to open synthetic textile market for first time. Current sales $1,800,000 per year.

NASHVILLE MACHINE TOOLS, INC., Nashville, Tenn. Largest manufacturer of turret lathes in the U.S. Sales $51,000,000.

Sales Supervisor, Detroit, Michigan (1965-1970)
Oversaw four salesmen and three service representatives primarily calling on automobile and auto parts manufacturers. Was responsible for a sales increase from $1,300,000 to $2,900,000.

Made first sales ever to business machine customer, who became third largest customer in country.

Salesman, Cleveland, Ohio (1962-1965)

Took over a territory whose sales never exceeded $275,000. Built it so that in the last four years sales were over $1,000,000 each year.

Education: E.  Indiana University, Bloomington, Indiana. B.S. in Mechanical Engineering, 1962. Varsity letter in baseball.

Personal:  Was raised in Elkhart, Indiana. Attended public schools. Was captain of high school baseball team.

Member:  Vice President, Sales Managers Institute of Fort Wayne. Assistant Chairman of every-member canvass for my church.

*The capital letters in this and the next resume refer to specific points made on pp. 102, and 103 under the heading "General Formats" below.

RESUME 6-2
Functional resume used to change careers

Note how it shows skills needed for a development officer's position, acquired in insurance agency management. Also this is a good example of the use of a summary to gain immediate favorable attention. A chronological resume would peg Harrison as an insurance sales manager with considerably less appeal for an organization seeking a fund raiser.

---

Frank J. Harrison
73 Glencove Street
Dallas, Texas
605-473-2954

### OBJECTIVE

A. DEVELOPMENT OFFICER responsible for planning, organizing, and conducting fund-raising programs, including deferred giving. Background includes:

B. Twenty five successful years in sales management and personal selling.
General Agent in Atlanta for major life insurance company.
President of national college alumni association.
Leadership experience as volunteer fund raiser.

### RELEVANT EXPERIENCE

C. SALES
MANAGEMENT

D. Planning, organizing, and managing marketing efforts of 15 full-time salesmen and 52 brokers . . . total sales consistently in top 15% among 65 agencies, including new agency record.

Leading annual giving campaigns in two churches, each with goal in excess of $100,000.

Organizing, promoting, and conducting regional conferences with nationally known speakers . . . setting up Washington trade association to advocate position with IRS and Congress.

Coordinating successful new product introduction program in 120 regional offices, using meeting outlines, printed brochures, and videotapes.

RESUME 6-2 *(continued)*

|  |  |
|---|---|
| **PERSONAL SELLING** | Initial life insurance sales earned leadership recognition . . . investment sales ranked 23d among 1,200 representatives. |
|  | Won regional trophy for exceeding quota of annuity sales . . . scored 84% gain in pension sales over previous period. |
|  | Developed systems using computer-prepared market data for individual prospect qualification and follow-through. |
|  | Successful joint selling to businessmen and professionals, working closely with accountants and attorneys. |
| **DEFERRED GIVING** | Technical Estate Planning field advisor in three different organizations, operating in six different states. |
|  | Chartered Life Underwriter (CLU) since 1954 . . . Certificate in Advanced Estate Planning (Texas), 1976. |
|  | Consulting with attorneys in the preparation of plan documents and amendments, including negotiating with the IRS to secure favorable tax treatment. |
|  | Conducting seminars and meetings covering technical aspects of capital transfers and estate conservation. |
| **ADMINIS-TRATION** | Responsible for systems and procedures covering $3,000,000 in annual collections from 8,800 customers, handled by clerical staff of 6. |
|  | Supervising administration of 120 pension and profit sharing plans . . . personally administering profit sharing plan with 47 participants and assets of $1,200,000. |

RESUME 6-2 *(concluded)*

---

Successfully redesigned unsatisfactory computerized accounting system to provide needed management information.

Creating and publishing weekly and monthly newsletters.

### PERSONAL HISTORY

E.  EMPLOYMENT

Pension Supervisor, North American Life Company. Responsible for all qualified plans in Dallas office (1974-    ).

Training Director, Multistates Insurance Company. Directed home office training schools for field management personnel (1972-1973).

Vice President, Brown, Smith, & Jones. Managed life department at Jacksonville headquarters (1966-1971).

General Agent, Wisconsin Life Company, Atlanta, GA. Responsible for sales, service, and office administration (1952-1965).

EDUCATION

BA Degree, Michigan State University.
MBA Program, University of Chicago.
CLU Degree, American College.

PERSONAL

Married, 5 children, ages 12-22.
Hobbies: Photography and skiing.
Excellent health.

---

logical resume is relatively inflexible, though, and it can emphasize shortcomings in your background. A functional resume allows a lot more flexibility in getting your story across and often can overcome major liabilities. The resume of Edward J. Ginsburg (Resume 6-3) is a special kind of resume called an *accomplishment resume.* It is one page and is basi-

RESUME 6-3
An accomplishment resume

A useful resume that emphasizes only the highlights. Good for blind prospecting.

Edward J. Ginsburg
75 Bancroft Court
Dallas, Texas 75934
375-942-8617

JOB OBJECTIVE: Assistant to President or financial officer in dynamic corporation or institution.

EDUCATION: Pomona College, 1959-1965 . . . Bachelor of Arts Degree.
Faworth University, Mendel University, 1966-1971 . . . accounting and investments.

EXPERIENCE:
1975-
Brooke Corporation, Boston, Massachusetts. Financial advisor and analyst for small asset management and family holding company.

1969-1975
Forester College, Dallas, Texas.
Assistant to the Treasurer, responsible for co-managing endowment fund including selection, purchase, and sale of securities. Coordinated deferred giving program.

1965-1969
Fort Worth Trust Company, Fort Worth, Texas.
Assistant to head of Trust Department, responsible for investment analysis and preparation of clients' tax returns.

ACCOMPLISHMENTS:
- Skilled in locating sources of permanent financing and working capital.
- Managed over $50 million of investments and co-managed an additional $90 million; performance superior to the market and most other institutions.
- Created a near riskless investment program designed to pay the bulk of expenses incurred in managing Forester's endowment.

RESUME 6-3 *(continued)*

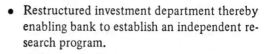

- Restructured investment department thereby enabling bank to establish an independent research program.

- Maintained tight rein on daily cash position thereby increasing annual income by more than $60,000.

- Helped administer and manage the investments of numerous trusts and estates.

STRENGTHS:  Able to handle a variety of tasks simultaneously, adept at working with people, persistent.

cally chronological. It hits only the major highlights, but it may have a better chance of being read completely in many situations than most, as it recognizes the reader's need to get as comprehensive a picture in as short a time as possible. This type of resume is very useful in a blind-prospecting type of campaign which will be discussed later. It emphasizes broad accomplishments—the individual's highest level of achievement, implying lots of lesser accomplishments.

The resumes of Goldberg (Resume 6-4), Shereshewski (Resume 6-5), and Flatley (Resume 6-6) are chronological resumes for a wide range of types of jobs. They are included to show how accomplishments can be included in resumes of people with widely varying backgrounds.

Judith Crane's functional resume (6-7) would be as effective if presented chronologically.

Samuel Fenton (Resume 6-8) used a functional resume that allowed for the in-depth presentation of certain accomplishments. Frances Lawson (Resume 6-9) used her functional resume to facilitate an in-depth description of hard-to-quantify

**RESUME 6-4**
Chronological resume of personnel specialist

Note accomplishment statements that are difficult to quantify.

---

Sandra J. Goldberg
57 North Street
Belleview, Texas  79432
(985) 374-8239


<u>Objective:</u>   Personnel Executive.


<u>1970-</u>       Southwestern Electronics Company, Houston, Texas.
           Manufacturer of semiconductors. Sales $24,000,000.
           1,100 employees.

           FRINGE BENEFIT ADMINISTRATOR (1975-     )
           Negotiated changes in our pension plan needed to conform
           to ERISA, working with our lawyer, actuary, and United
           Electrical Workers.

           Developed fringe benefit pamphlet outlining principal pro-
           visions of all plans for employees. Received favorable com-
           ment from Union president.

           Initiated annual fringe benefit review for keeping supervisors
           current on all benefit changes and interpretation problems.
           Reduced delay in getting annual actuary report from 11 to 6
           months.

           WAGE AND SALARY ADMINISTRATOR (1973-1974)
           Standardized procedure for updating evaluation of new and
           revised jobs. Eliminated 6-month backlog of jobs waiting for
           evaluation.

           Improved reliability of wage and salary surveys in our area.
           Found numerous errors in prior surveys, all conducted by
           mail, then supplemented mail surveys with personal review.

           Computerized wage and salary reviews so supervisor alerted
           to review data and normal increase on each employee.

**RESUME 6-4** *(continued)*

---

> PERSONNEL RECRUITER (1970-1973)
> Reduced backlog of unfilled technical jobs by over 2/3 in a period of increasing shortage by getting engineers to visit college campuses with me.
>
> Developed minority recruiting program which resulted in our having highest % of minority employment and one of lowest turnover rates in the city among major employers. This involved recruiting in minority areas in the city, arranging transportation, and developing broad indoctrination program.
>
> Education:   Maryland State, Baltimore, MD—AB in Psychology, 1970; Secretary of College dramatic club. Active in College social work program.
>
> Personal:   Married, 2 children.  Good health.
>
> Interests:   Church choir. Photography. Camping.

---

**RESUME 6-5**
Chronological resume of engineer

Here again, see some of the ways of showing accomplishments where quantifying them isn't easy.

---

> William J. Shereshewski
> 437 Madden Lane
> Atlanta, Georgia 37942
>
>
> Objective:   Electronics Project Engineer
>
> Experience:
>
> 1971-   Digital General Resources, Atlanta, Georgia
>
> Manufacturer of optical recognition systems.
> Sales $23,000,000; 900 employees.
>
> DIGITAL LOGIC DESIGN ENGINEER

---

RESUME 6-5 *(continued)*

Designed and built a precision computer controller CRT flying spot scanner for collecting information from film. This system resulted in a saving of $27,000 the first year.

Designed more than ten servo systems including film drives with varied performance goals.

Increased the uptime of a large commercially-operated computer complex by 50%, increasing the confidence of the customers and adding 27% to the revenue of the equipment.

Proposed and designed a digital programmer that led to many repeat contracts. This system has been in use for over two years.

Automated a major laboratory reducing cost by 15% and increasing revenue by $67,000 per year.

Education: Mississippi Polytechnic Institute, BS in Electrical Engineering, 1971. Treasurer of MPI Weekly Journal.

Summer Employment: Precision Plastics, Birmingham, Alabama
1970—Stock chaser
1969—Shipping Platform

Grandview Camp, Benton, Mississippi
1968—Counselor

Personal: Single. Good health.

Interests: Photography, flying, basketball.

**RESUME 6-6**
Chronological resume of a stockbroker

It shows a wide variety of accomplishments in addition to a good sales record. The image of a creative, aggressive salesman comes across.

---

JAMES L. FLATLEY
76 High Hill Road
New Canaan, Connecticut
(203)547-3284


objective        INVESTMENTS

business         INSTITUTIONAL SALESMAN, RAYMOND RANDOLPH,
experience       NEW YORK

1969-            Developed more than $30,000 of profitable commission
present          business with two large institutions that the firm had never
                 done business with before.

                 Increased by 1,000% the amount of commission revenues
                 received from two other large billion dollar institutions.

                 Initiated the idea of getting our research analysts to come
                 from Boston on a more regular basis to see New York
                 security analysts.

                 Started the program of bringing company managements to
                 New York seminars and luncheons with our security
                 analysts.

1965-1969        RETAIL SALES MANAGER & ASSISTANT OFFICE
                 MANAGER, DIAMOND SECURITIES, NEW YORK

                 Tripled the revenues and profits of the New York office.

                 Recruited and trained several top security salesmen, one of
                 whom became the firm's leading producer with commission
                 revenues of $300,000 per year.

                 Increased advertising and sales leads from 1 or so per month
                 to more than 100 per week, primarily through the tele-
                 phone market report which I devised.

---

RESUME 6-6 *(continued)*

Developed and implemented an imaginative advertising program that made the name "Diamond Securities" familiar to investors.

**1957-1965** SECURITIES SALESMAN, KNOX & SPRING, PHILADELPHIA, PENNSYLVANIA

Initiated the program to bring Union Pension Fund business to the firm, and succeeded in getting thousands of dollars of commission business from Philadelphia's largest local union pension fund.

Succeeded in convincing wealthy individuals, a large insurance company, and a prominent law firm to again do business with Knox & Spring.

Sold more mutual funds and municipal bonds than any other salesman.

Developed more business with institutions in Worcester than the firm had done before.

**1956** PART-TIME SALESMAN, KEITH & SHAW, DETROIT, MICHIGAN

Swamped the firm with such a large order for cushions that they had to triple their manufacturing output.

**other management experience**

**1970-1976**

SCHOOL COMMITTEEMAN, NEW CANAAN, CONNECTICUT

Initiated the "program budget" for the entire school system so that we would know how much each program was costing the taxpayer.

Provided a summer school program for 1,200 children that did not cost the taxpayers any additional money.

Established throughout the school system a comprehensive method to evaluate each teacher, school, and program.

Cut the number of hours involved in lengthy negotiations by over 80%.

RESUME 6-6 *(concluded)*

|  |  |
|---|---|
|  | Led the committee in a new direction that enabled us to get Town Meeting approval for a badly needed addition at the High School. |
|  | Changed the School Committee's reputation with the press from a negative one to a positive one. |
| **1952-1955** | SUPPLY OFFICER, U.S. NAVY, aboard various ships at sea. |
|  | Developed a more efficient system of paying the crew aboard an aircraft carrier that resulted in savings of over 6,000 man-hours per month. |
|  | Doubled the profits of the Ship's Store so that more benefits could be made available to the crew. |
| **education** | NORTHWESTERN, EVANSTON, ILLINOIS |
| **1955-1957** | MBA degree in June 1957. Specialized in marketing and finance. Upper third of class. Expenses financed by stock market profits and G.I. Bill. |
|  | UNIVERSITY OF DETROIT, DETROIT, MICHIGAN |
| **1948-1952** | B.S. degree in June 1952. Majored in General Business and other courses in General Engineering and Naval Science. Graduated first in NROTC Supply Corps class and upper quarter of University. Financed expenses with NROTC scholarship and part-time employment. |
| **community activities** | Former Chairman, Republican Finance Committee, New Canaan, Connecticut. |
|  | Former Chairman, Finance Committee of the Trinitarian Congregational Church, New Canaan, Connecticut. |
| **personal** | Married, 4 children, excellent health. |
| **interests** | Hunting, fishing, camping. |

**RESUME 6-7**
Functional resume for college administrator

Use of similar presentation of accomplishments for nonbusiness background. She could have just as effectively used a chronological resume.

Judith B. Crane
97 Yonkers Avenue
Bronxville, New York
(212) 437-9438

### OBJECTIVE

Administrator in Higher Education

Background includes: 14 successful years in administration of higher education with 6 years in admissions. Dean and Vice President of private University (3,500 undergraduate and 6,500 graduate and continuing education students). Significant background in Fine and Applied Arts.

### RELEVANT EXPERIENCE

**Administration** Responsible for program and development, systems, and procedures covering $1.7 million of annual operating budget, handled by 45 professional and support staff.

Reduced student attrition from 23% to 8% in two years by improved counseling and introducing 12 new programs.

Was 1 of 3 key members of the President's staff which increased the size of the University by 110% in 10 years.

Initiated University summer Orientation Program for entering students and their parents.

Computerized course scheduling and student academic records.

**Admissions** Planning, organizing, and managing marketing efforts of 7 full-time admissions personnel . . . increased recruitment annually from 1,100 to 1,700. Geographical origin rose from 29 states and 21 foreign countries to 48 states and 53 foreign countries.

RESUME 6-7 *(continued)*

Coordinated successful new educational introduction program in college fairs, using unique brochures and videotapes. Developed multimedia show for national conferences and on-sight recruitment.

Developed first system of using our alumni for recruitment of students in all 50 states and in 23 foreign countries.

**Teaching experience**  Extensive background in English—developed and taught creative writing courses in prep school for regular school year and in intensive summer program, and for college summer school—also developed advanced placement course in prep school in English literature.

### PERSONAL HISTORY

**Employment**  Vice President for Student Affairs, University of Yonkers (1974-present).

Dean of Students, University of Yonkers (1971-1974).

Director of Admissions, University of Yonkers (1967-1971).

Assistant Director of Admissions, University of Yonkers (1962-1967).

Dean of Admissions, Baltimore Academy, Baltimore, Maryland (1958-1962).

English Teacher, Baltimore Academy (1955-1958).

**Education**  B.A. Degree, 1953, University of Pittsburgh
M.A. Degree, 1955, University of Cincinnati

**Personal**  Married, three children, excellent health. Interests include: books, theatre, travel, sports, and church-related activities.

**RESUME 6-8**
A functional resume to show certain experience in depth

His background probably could have been just as effectively presented in a chronological resume, because of his increasingly favorable record in one field. Note how this style allows for in-depth description of his experience in certain areas, while presenting a brief overall summary of highlights. While in excess of normal length of two pages, this format has proved effective in direct contact with employers.

---

Samuel Fenton
37 Primrose Street
Far Pond, Connecticut  05392
203-604-0111


Objective: Production Management

Some of my accomplishments in my 19 years of experience, currently as Plant Manager (see detailed descriptions later):

Cost Savings

Introduced a competitive bidding system on major purchases that saved $2,550,000 in 2 years.

Redesigned key component and tooling which reduced scrap loss from 27% to 3% at an annual saving of $175,000.

Improved Utilization of Space

My program of improved inventory management and warehousing methods eliminated the need for a 52% expansion of space at a cost of $1,710,000.

Redesigned Product Line

Eliminated costly unneeded features in redesign of product line representing 16% of sales. These changes were instrumental in bringing it from breakeven to 6% profit level.

Introduced Planned Maintenance Program

My program of preventive maintenance, project scheduling, and work sampling enabled us to reduce downtime from 6% to 3% at the same time reducing maintenance cost annually by $135,000.

RESUME 6-8 *(continued)*

---

Job History

1973-        Plant Manager, Electronic Postage Meters, Inc., Racine,
             Wisconsin

1968-1973    Superintendent, Electronic Postage Meters, Inc.

1964-1968    Assistant Superintendent, General Dynamics, Riverside,
             California

1962-1964    Chief Tool Engineer, General Dynamics, Riverside, California

1956-1962    Tool Engineer, General Electric, Bayside, California

Education

BS in Mechanical Engineering, University of Michigan, 1956.

Professional Memberships

American Society of Tool Engineers

Personal

Married, 2 children, good health.
Chairman, every-member canvass of my church.
Golf, fishing, coin collecting.

Achieved Savings of $2,550,000 in Purchases on Revised Purchasing
Procedures

Our purchases of sodium hexachlorate had been averaging 1,200,000
pounds at 37¾ cents per pound and had always been from a single source.

A new project required a sixfold expansion of this material. I arranged
for the solicitation of bids from five other sources.

The lowest bid which met our quality requirements was at 19½ cents
per pound. In the second year our requirements were 7,400,000 pounds
resulting in a savings of over $1,350,000 in this year alone.

This experience brought out much wider use of competitive bidding in
the company. Similar experiences were achieved on a number of key materials. Total savings from the revised procedures were $1,200,000.

RESUME 6-8 *(concluded)*

Redesigned Key Component and Tooling

Our new line of electronic postage meters had fallen three months behind schedule. A major factor was our aluminum housing cracking around two very tricky contours. Scrap losses were running 29% and our supplier couldn't keep up with demand.

I devised a redesign of the component and the necessary tooling. The several meetings I had with our Chief Tooling Engineer, our Senior Design Engineer, and our supplier's Plant Manager organized the design changes. Within five weeks these changes were put into operation. Scrap losses were down to 7% two weeks later and to 3% within a month. At the end of seven months production was back on our original schedule and we were realizing savings in scrap losses of $175,000.

Improved Utilization of Space

Our 105,000-square-foot warehouse was overloaded when we added our new postage meter line. Management was considering a proposal for an expansion of 52% at a cost of $1,710,000.

I carefully surveyed the turnover of all items and found that over one third of them were being ordered in larger quantities than needed. This led to more economical production runs and lower space requirements. A new type of pallet more suitable to our products was discovered which enabled us to increase palletizing over 35%. At my urging our sales department increased our consignment terms to dealers reducing the time needed for our warehousing them.

As a result of these steps, we found that we already had adequate space for our needs.

RESUME 6-9
Resume to present hard-to-measure accomplishments

Lawson had good experience as an administrative assistant. However, her experience couldn't point to great accomplishments (i.e., cost savings, etc.). This functional resume allowed her to present her major skills in much more depth than could be done effectively in a chronological resume.

---

FRANCES LAWSON
89 Beacon Street
New Haven, Connecticut 06321
(203) 497-8534

Objective:  Administrative Assistant–Financial Analyst–Economic Writer

Among my skills developed in 15 years, most recently as Administrative Assistant to a Vice President of one of the largest and most highly respected investment counselors, Wall Street Management & Research Company:

Investment Research

Analyzed research reports on various companies and made recommendations on whether their stock should be sold, bought, or held. Analyzed customers' portfolios and made recommendations on changes that should be made. Analyzed make-up and performance of our mutual-fund portfolios with competition, making recommendations for corrective action.

Financial Analysis

Projected cash income for portfolios under management, including estimating future dividend levels. Set up schedules on maturities of debt issues. Prepared cash forecasts.

Economic Reporting

Participated for my firm at economic and investment meetings in various parts of the country with officials of many of the best-known national investment firms. Reported the results with recommendations to top management.

Office Management

Handled the day-to-day supervision of an office of 14. Was responsible for assignment and quality of work. Interviewed applicants for jobs. Reviewed performance of staff and made recommendations for salary increases.

**RESUME 6-9** *(continued)*

---

Work Experience

1976-present    Bowman & Schyller, Investment Counsellors—Staff Assistant

1960-1975      Wall Street Management & Research Company—Administrative Assistant

1957-1959      American Cyanamid Company—Executive Secretary

Education

Mason Franklin College, Cedarville, Ohio: B.A. Degree. College Glee Club
New Haven University 1-year Security Analysts Course

Personal

Volunteer worker—American Red Cross, New Haven United Fund

---

skills. Peter Carey (Resume 6-10) shows profit and nonprofit experience. Functional resumes can be organized by:

> Function (for a sales supervisor, for example, sales, training, new ideas).
>
> Personal attributes (leadership, imagination, details).
>
> Skills (problem solving, goal setting, motivating people).

**General formats**

Let's examine the general format of a chronological and a functional resume in more depth to see how each can be constructed most effectively. First a chronological resume (see William S. Morrison, Resume 6-1) shows:

A. Job objective: Here is the first thing that most readers see—a simple statement of what kind of a job is being sought. This answers the first question an employer has on his or her mind, "What kind of job is this person looking for?"

**RESUME 6-10**
A functional resume for senior executive for a nonprofit organization

Note how experiences in a number of quite different jobs are pulled together toward one objective.

---

Peter G. Carey
Noonan Road
Denver, CO
Bus: 715-843-7917
Res: 715-639-7948

FINANCIAL AND ADMINISTRATIVE EXECUTIVE with more than 24 years' experience in gaining permanent control over financial and administrative operating problems in both profit and nonprofit organizations. Major strengths include:

Developing solutions to operating problems, then managing the implementation of corrective action with measurable bottom-line results;
Communicating clearly with all levels of management, as well as with professional staff and clients, on the specific goals and objectives to be achieved;
Establishing ongoing systems, controls, and computerized management information systems.

### SELECTED ACHIEVEMENTS

| | |
|---|---|
| MANAGING TURNAROUND SITUATIONS | Took leadership role in changing 15 year record of operating losses ($1.7 million in 1972) to an operating gain of $405,000 in 1973 for a highly complex major nonprofit institution. Helped increase investment portfolio from $900,000 to $3.6 million during that period by redirecting philanthropy into capital reserves. . . . Earlier achieved a one-time 35% annual increase in departmental profitability, some $1.6 million, by reducing a major financial institution's mutual funds shareholder accounting backlog by 75% in six months and establishing daily processing of incoming work. |
| ORGANIZING AND DIRECTING | Recruited, directed, and integrated new management team for nonprofit institution's 140-person |

RESUME 6-10 *(continued)*

|  | financial department, plus temporary consultants in computers, hospital reimbursement, pensions, and insurance, as well as a new auditing firm in order to facilitate the turnaround.... Earlier recruited, directed and integrated new management team, re-organized 225-person shareholder accounting department in major financial institution, and temporarily recruited two consulting firms to establish controls plus review and correct several thousand backlogged shareholder accounts. |
| --- | --- |
| COMMUNICATING EFFECTIVELY | Convinced management and professional staff of nonprofit institution to support programs for achieving balanced financial results and channeling philanthropy into capital uses. Enabled management and professional staff to comprehend more fully an intricate financial structure through publishing clear, comprehensive, and timely financial reports. .... Earlier converted a previously antagonistic mutual funds client management into cooperative team players, who then helped significantly with irate shareholder complaints and offered suggestions for improvement, by thoroughly involving them as the shareholder accounting backlog was being brought under control. |
| COMPUTER SYSTEMS | Reduced ratio of receivables to revenues by 25% by installing institution's first computerized billing and receivables system to handle over $35 million in annual billings. Clearly identified major areas of operating losses through introducing a new computerized chart of accounts and general ledger system. Computerized for the first time and gained control over all major financial systems, powered by IBM 370/145 hardware with over 65 on-line terminals and making possible many of the "selected achievements" being described. |
| BUDGET CONTROL | Instituted responsibility budgeting system throughout 4,300 employee nonprofit institution, the con- |

RESUME 6-10 *(concluded)*

|                  | trol from which helped produce a 1977 operating gain $450,000 better than budget contrasted to a presystem 1972 loss $1.9 million poorer than plan. |
|------------------|-----|
| PROBLEM SOLVING  | Increased sluggish sales of a specialized industrial product by 42% in first year and to over $500,000 the second year through a targeted quality improvement and sales promotion program. . . . Later reduced annual $300,000 operating losses of an overseas banking subsidiary by some 20% by realistically assessing European market potential and convincing overseas and domestic management to redirect and scale down the business. |

### BUSINESS RECORD

<u>Chief Financial Officer,</u> Denver General Hospital, Denver, CO, 1974 to
present.
Director of Fiscal Services in a $65 million institution engaged in patient
care, teaching, research, and certain commercial activities.

<u>Vice President, Planning & Development;</u> previously <u>Vice President, Fund
Manager,</u> Denver Corp., Mutual Funds Division, Denver, 1968-74.
Managed large shareholder accounting department, helped redirect newly
established European subsidiary, assembled strategic business plan for the
division.

<u>Director of Planning,</u> Franklin Motor Company, Denver, 1964-68.
Developed and helped implement first corporate strategic business plan
for this $30 million business.

Cheyenne Metals Co., Cheyenne, WY, 1957-64.
  <u>Divisional Product Manager/Advertising and Sales Promotion Manager,</u>
  1962-64.
  <u>Divisional Quality Control/Production Control Manager,</u> 1959-62.

<u>Production Control Manager,</u> The Firth Company, Ft. Collins, CO,
1957-59.

| EDUCATION | AB with Honors, Colorado University, 1952. |
|-----------|--------------------------------------------|
| PERSONAL  | Married, 2 children; Ht. 6' 0"; Wt. 175 lbs.; Excellent health. |

**RESUME 6-11**
A functional resume to change from a military career to industry

Note the language used in industry to describe military experience and the emphasis on the skills most likely needed in the type of job he is seeking. A chronological resume would have played up his military career and made it difficult to project these skills. A resume written in military terminology would turn civilian employers off.

---

Francis L. Townsend
294 Suffolk Street
Valley Forge, Pennsylvania 39427
(615) 939-4322

| | |
|---|---|
| **Objective** | Financial Management |
| **Summary** | Columbia School of Business, MBA, 1977<br>Fifteen years of administrative, diplomatic, and command experience.<br>Strong background in budgeting, long-range planning, cost reduction, facilities management, auditing and negotiations.<br>Lt. Colonel (Retired), U.S. Army.<br>West Point graduate. |
| **Financial Planning** | Responsible for the consolidation of the budgets of 23 major military activities totaling about $100,000,000 and involving 20,000 in personnel, and the negotiating of their reductions to a prescribed figure. Involved in this were budgets for major capital expenditures and a variety of new programs. |
| **Cost Reduction** | Devised a system which eliminated the need for over $900,000 in heavy equipment purchases.<br><br>Developed and sold the overall plan which resulted in a 10% (2,000 people) reduction in our activity's budget.<br><br>Initiated and executed a program which resulted in a 10% increase in the writing and production of training manuals, while keeping the budget constant at $2,000,000. |

RESUME 6-11 *(continued)*

| | |
|---|---|
| **Negotiations &** **Investigations** | Led a small team to review the capabilities of several major military installations in Vietnam and their needs in case of escalation. |
| | Conducted a study for the U.S. Military Mission of the long-range personnel needs of the Greek Army. |
| | Was one of 21 international military officers in a UN mission to report on the status of the Ethiopian-Somalia War. Was appointed mission representative to the Government of Saudi Arabia. |
| **Languages** | French—good; Greek—fair. |
| **Personal** | Married, 2 children. |

**RESUME 6-12**
Functional resume for a job hopper

Note the emphasis on accomplishments and the playing down of employment history.

Natalie Arhanian
9 Duncan Road
Frankfurt, KY 07513
Office: 431-797-8433
Home: 431-295-7482

**resume**

**Objective:** MARKETING OPERATIONS SUPPORT, to help with new business and retain existing customers.

**Qualified by:** Fourteen years' sales and marketing experience in the electronics and other industries. Able to communicate effectively with executives as well as technical leaders. Strong orientation to customer service.

**Related achievements:** Planned and coordinated a five-year growth program. Result was a 600% increase in sales to $19,000,000 and a tenfold increase in profits.

Coordinated the recruiting, training, and placement of sixty sales representatives and branch managers. Made improvements to sales compensation plans. Sales productivity rose to $160,000 per man per year from $90,000.

Developed cost control program for marketing operation of a $20 million company, which resulted in an additional profit contribution of $1 million.

Developed and managed a range of marketing operations including: order processing, delivery planning, credit approvals, advertising, and publications. Orders processed increased to 7,000 annually from 100. Sales leads totaled over 100,000/year.

Expanded sales by $5 million annually with no significant increase in costs. Prepared pricing proposals and negotiated annual sales agreements with major corporations and the federal government.

RESUME 6-12 *(continued)*

In computer system sales, was the leader of a team that closed $500,000 of orders in five months. The next $550,000 are in negotiations.

As a consultant to a major bank, developed the marketing package to sell time on its computer systems for security trading and fund transfers. Increased the revenue potential 30% to $1.3 million per year.

Developed a joint venture with a multi-unit nursing home group. Increased time-sharing service income from $5,000 to $10,000 per month by the sale of low-cost management reports and third-party billing procedures.

Evaluated the price, performance, delivery, and product service offered by nine leading minicomputer manufacturers.

Identified product and marketing changes that helped increase sales 12% a year for two years.

Coordinated the market introduction, scheduled production, and developed the prices for the introduction of a word-processing machine.

**Employment History:**

MARKETING MANAGER, Farnsworth Computer Corporation. Developer of computer-based business systems for inventory management, general accounting, order processing, cash management, and financial reporting. Sixty employees (1976-date).

MARKETING MANAGER, Baker Management Systems, Inc. Time-sharing service and computer software firm. Thirty-five employees (1975-1976).

MARKETING CONSULTANT, Eliot Corporation. Textbook publishers. Sales $35,000,000 (1974-1975).

PROGRAM MANAGER, International Marketing, Gloucester Corporation. Manufacturer of electronic components. Sales $17,000,000 (1973-1974).

RESUME 6-12 *(concluded)*

|  |  |
|---|---|
|  | MARKETING DIRECTOR, Resources Funding Corporation. Industrial park and shopping center developer (1971-1973).<br><br>PRODUCT MARKETING MANAGER, Gardner Electronics, Inc. Manufacturer of computer components, 700 employees (1966-1971). |
| **Education:** | MBA, Michigan State University. Major: Marketing and Control. Member, Marketing Club.<br><br>AB, Hancock College, Major: Mathematics. Mansfield Foundation scholarship. |
| **Personal:** | Single—health excellent.<br>Incorporator, Fairfield County Savings Bank.<br>Member of Frankfurt Historical Commission. |

B. A simple description of each company Morrison worked for including the type of company and approximate size.

C. A simple statement about each of his positions, how long he held them, and a summary of his responsibilities in them.

D. A series of statements outlining positive accomplishments that he made on each job.

E. For an executive who has been working for many years, education should be stated after work experience. On the other hand, for someone who has been working only a few years, and particularly if a person has an outstanding education, it should be shown right under the job objective. For an experienced executive, putting education near the start indicates too prominent an emphasis on the education as contrasted with work experience.

A summary is called for in part B of the functional resume described below. This can be used in a chronological resume, but it is of much less importance when the writer has a more conventional job record.

Some highlights of a typical functional resume are shown in Frank J. Harrison's (Resume 6-2):

A.  Again the objective is stated right at the start.
B.  Because Harrison's major selling points are scattered throughout his experience, including a summary focuses the reader's immediate attention on his most favorable experience.
C.  Here is a key function that is required for the job. Note the wide latitude that is given to this designation.
D.  Here is a series of accomplishment statements that relate to the particular function.
E.  As explained above, an employment history should be included which highlights the dates worked, the particular companies, job titles, and a description of each company.

Selecting the most effective type is your first major resume decision.

**Your resume and first impressions**

An employer's decision on your resume may result from a few first impressions. What job do you want? What are your principal assets—particularly as they relate to the key requirements of the job you're seeking (see "Your Job Description," in Chapter Four). Display them prominently. What are your major liabilities? Play them down. The first two thirds of your resume's first page is the *critical zone.* This is where your initial (and often the lasting) impression is made. Make sure it includes your objectives and your major assets. Let's see how initial impressions can create liabilities for certain job hunters.

Bill Reardon had been chief financial officer (CFO) of a large college for two years and he was determined to get back into industry, where he had spent 10 years as CFO. Yet the entire first page of his resume described his college experience—and much of it was unique to a college. Bill found himself pegged as a college financial executive. A different emphasis—starting off with an experience summary and using a functional resume—highlighted his 12 years of solid accomplishments as a top financial officer (the last two years of which were spent at a college) and made a much more effective resume for him.

Francis Townsend (Resume 6-11) was an army Lt. colonel who retired after 20 years and then got his MBA. His problem was to get a civilian employer to accept his military administrative, diplomatic, and command experience as comparable to what he might have gained in industry. His original (chronological) resume, worded in military terms and with his MBA education buried at the end, gave the impression of an experienced military officer with no particular business credentials. When he switched to a functional resume (worded in business terms), emphasizing his recent MBA and his 20 years' experience, he quite quickly secured an interview which resulted in a position as assistant treasurer of a $0.5-billion company.

Natalie Arhanian (Resume 6-12) was a $30,000-a-year marketing manager who had numerous jobs in a few years. Naturally she was very concerned about her image as a job hopper. Yet her original (chronological) resume's first page listed every recent job so that the image she was trying to avoid was emphasized. Her good record of achievements was buried on the second page, and most readers never bothered to read it. A functional resume developing interest at the start with her successful achievements, and with her job history near the end, made a much more positive impression.

Ed Fisher for several years had import and export positions with two companies, after four years of setting sales and profits records in his role as chief operating officer of an 8,000-employee foreign subsidiary. Although this latter experience was his strongest, it didn't appear until almost the bottom of the second page of his chronological resume. Therefore, it probably wouldn't be seen by most employers because they would put his resume in the "not interested" pile before they finished the first page. Including this outstanding experience in a summary at the start gave it immediate impact.

Subtlety can also help. For example, someone seeking a plant superintendent's position might project primarily as a production-planning specialist. Or a candidate for a controller's position doesn't include computer and reporting systems revision experience. The way to project your most favorable image is to construct your resume so you appear to fit the description for your preferred job, that is, the ideal candidate. Emphasize your strongest experience. Minimize your weakest.

"Separated"—"Age 50" were two of the items in the heading of Esther Emerson's resume. What kind of an impression do you think they made? They weren't necessary at all—so why were they included?

Review each of the resumes included here. Ask yourself, What are the candidates' two or three major strengths? Their weaknesses? Does the particular format make a particularly favorable presentation of each candidate's qualifications? Then ask yourself: (1) What are my major strengths and weaknesses? (2) What form of resume best presents my qualifications?

**Is your objective clear?**     Since most employers seek specialists, your resume should state your objective simply and right off. You'll greatly reduce your ability to sell yourself as a specialist if you haven't a reasonable answer to the key question, What do you want to do?

But what if you have two different objectives? You may not be able to decide between the two until you've actually interviewed for each. Don't include two incompatible objectives in your resume—for example, position in finance or marketing. Marketing executives are looking for people experienced in marketing, finance executives in finance. If you are at a stage in your campaign where you still have two widely differing objectives, make up two resumes, each tailored to a different objective.

Can you leave off the objective in the resume but specify it in a covering letter, for instance, in answer to an ad? Here you run the risk that the letter won't get a careful reading or becomes separated as your resume is passed around. Furthermore, such a resume can't be as effective as one you've tailored to a specific job. Remember, the cost of printing is a pretty small item.

Objectives that are too general are usually worse than no objectives at all:

> "A challenging, people-oriented, problem-solving position requiring the creative use of resources and opportunities."

> "Challenging position offering growth potential and the opportunity to effectively use diverse administrative experience."

Effective job objectives can be worded in a variety of ways. The main characteristic of good ones is that they clearly indicate the type of job you're seeking. Some effective objectives are:

Production management.

Financial or administrative management in a company where there is a need for improvement of financial planning, control, and profit-planning techniques.

(Note that beyond "management" little is added.)

School administration with particular emphasis on budgeting and long-range planning.

Sales or Marketing Management.

Development Engineering, particularly field testing of prototypes.

A less effective objective would be:

Vice President Finance or Treasurer (this may preclude some good opportunities, as employers may think you're interested only in these particular jobs. "Senior Financial Management" covers the same jobs, but it is broader).

If you start out with a broad objective and later decide to narrow it considerably, revise your resume accordingly.

**Focus on accomplishments**

You may show your experience by listing all the functions you're responsible for:

"Responsible for all production processes and assembly, production planning, plant maintenance, production methods, and tool engineering."

What this statement doesn't show is how effectively you carried out your responsibilities. A series of accomplishment statements, one on each principal function of your job, not only will show you held the responsibility, but also how well you carried it out.

Fair: "Initiated the changeover from individual final assembly of our smallest screw machines to assembling them on a continuous line."

Good: "Oversaw the installation of assembly line techniques on our smallest screw machines, which saved $175,000 a year."

Sometimes you can't put numbers on your achievements, but they still can be worded more effectively:

Poor: "Recruited and trained 300 people."

Good: "In a very tight labor market recruited over 300 technical personnel. Developed training programs which rapidly upgraded needed skills. Increased minorities from 1 percent to 5 percent. Achieved lowest turnover locally in our industry."

Poor: "Wrote Purchasing Department procedure manual."

Good: "Developed first Purchasing Department policy and procedure manual. Researched current practices in Purchasing and related departments. Recommended many changes. Reconciled many differences of opinion. Got final approval of Vice President and Purchasing Agent."

If a major accomplishment was as a part of a team effort, write "Played a key role in . . ." or "Was a member of a team which . . . ." Your PAR writeups make writing your accomplishments much easier. Describing your accomplishments in this way means you have stated the responsibilities of your job at the same time. Don't bury your accomplishments on a separate page—show some key ones in the critical zone.

**Preparing your resume**

Since the preparation of a top-notch resume takes time, prepare a temporary one at the very start of your campaign. By doing this, you will have a resume that can be used until you have a really good one ready.

To prepare your final resume, start with name, address, objective, and then state military, educational, and personal background. Next prepare employment statistics: dates, companies worked for, titles, and so on. Now comes the major variable—your detailed experience—accomplishments, background on companies, specific jobs, and the like. In the first draft, put in everything you may want in your final draft. Don't worry about the length, format, and so on, at this time. Get it typed.

Set the draft aside for two or three days. Then aim to get your resume down to proper length. How do you reduce a three-page draft to two? A small part of the excess can be eliminated by reducing margins, type style, and the like—but you may pay a great price in readability. Practically the whole reduction must be in content—by eliminating low priority items and by getting the same ideas across (often more effectively) in fewer words. Use short words, crisp sentences. Avoid the passive voice. Compare your wording with accomplishment statements shown in most of the resumes included here.

Once you have the proper length (with few exceptions, two pages are maximum), zero in on the format. Make sure the things that you want to get attention stand out—your objective, your key qualifications. By use of indentations, capital letters, short paragraphs, numbers (use numerals, not words), you can get your message across most effectively.

Finally, use the questions at the end of this chapter as a checklist, with particular emphasis on how effectively your credentials show you're qualified for the job you're seeking.

*Specifics to include*

*Business experience*—The detail should come from your accomplishments (Chapter Five).

*Education*—Include your graduate school, college—your most important first. You may want to include courses applicable to your job goal. State your degree, any academic honors or awards, amount of expenses earned, your major (if relevant). If you graduated within the past ten years, include offices in extracurricular organizations. If you have an outstanding recent academic record, stating that may be most effective right after your objective. Omit your high school unless you've had less than four years of experience.

*Military*—List your branch of service, rank at discharge, and commendations. A couple of lines will suffice unless this experience is a major part of your recent career.

*Business and community organizations*—List the organizations and your official capacity. Don't forget to include major organizations you're no longer affiliated with.

*Personal*—Include one or two lines of hobbies, particularly any related to your job goal. This shows you as a well-rounded person and one of the items may develop rapport with a prospective employer.

*Publications, languages, inventions*—List any you have.

If you have any No's in your answers to the questions in this section, revise your resume accordingly.

**Some questions to ask yourself in critiquing your resume**

Answer each of the following questions after carefully thinking about it in relation to your resume.

|  |  | Yes | No |
|---|---|---|---|

1. *Have you carefully evaluated whether a chronological or functional resume is best for you?*

2. *Does your resume clearly answer the most important questions readers will ask themselves?* What is your job objective? Why are you a good candidate for such a position?

3. *Are the three or four most important items of your background clearly shown in the critical zone?* Have you played down your principal liabilities (if any)? If chronological, are your last five years' experience (what an employer is most interested in) adequately emphasized?

4. *Is the bias shown in your resume oriented to an employer's likely needs?* Have you shown positive accomplishments in almost all of the principal functions you'd be expected to have for the job? Does your experience imply you have almost all of the personal attributes required? Compare your resume carefully with your job description.

5. *Do your accomplishment statements start with action words?*

6. *Do they include measuring sticks of accomplishment* (numbers, qualifying adjectives, etc.)?

7. *Are you getting all the mileage you can out of your accomplishments?*

8. *Is the length of your resume right?* Ask yourself, does an ad with a lot of text have more impact on you than one with less that tells you what you need to know? A two-page resume should be sufficient. If you have a long and truly outstanding record, three pages is permissible. A one-page resume can also be effective in the blind-prospecting phase of your campaign. If it's too long, be selective in what you present and work on the wording. Read "The Broadcast Letter" (Chapter Eight)

*Yes*   *No*

to see how a number of ideas are written in a few words. Look at the applicant's first accomplishment statement: "Since 1972, increased sales almost 40% (sales up $2.0 million) with 1976 profits up $280,000 over 1972, when I became vice president." In this short sentence there are three distinct selling points: increased sales, increased profits, and promotion to vice president.

9. *If chronological, does your record show increasing responsibilities and accomplishments?*

10. *Have you excluded unreasonable restrictions on your job* such as "Location—New York City area"? Including any restrictions might make a poor impression on employers in other areas at a time when you want to make the most favorable impression possible. As opportunities develop, you can impose such a limitation when you evaluate offers.

11. *Does the concluding date on your resume imply that you are working?* Don't show "1974-present year." Show "1974-present" or "1974-    ." Use present tense when talking about your latest position. "Assistant Production Manager." Not "Was Assistant Production Manager."

12. *Do the names of the companies you've worked for and your job titles describe the scope of your responsibilities?* Don't assume employers will recognize the name and size of a company, particularly in this era of mergers. Something like "United Conglomerate (formerly XYZ Corp.)" may be needed to clarify it.

13. *Does the title of your job fully describe your responsibilities?* Executive Vice President was the title of the chief operating officer of XYZ—Italy. His boss was located in Paris and called V.P. European Operations (and President—Italy, President—Northern Europe, etc.). Why not use Chief Executive Officer (as Executive Vice President)—XYZ—Italy?

14. *Have you described your experience in simple understandable language?* Short sentences? Forceful, but

simple, words? Absence of technical jargon—are you
sure readers will understand or like to communicate
using these words? Are any abbreviations universally
known? Make sure proper names are understood—
"Holland Prize" means little—"Holland Prize (awarded
to three seniors for outstanding scholarship and leadership)" tells a lot. Review the resume samples and see the
simplicity of the writing—short sentences, simple words.     ____      ____

15. *Does your resume have eye appeal?* Type that's easy to
    read? Is it uncluttered? You probably will have more
    impact with four 2-line paragraphs than 12 lines of
    densely packed type.                                     ____      ____

16. *Have you differentiated in typing between your com-
    pany, your division, and your position?* You want each
    to have immediate impact. If you don't show each typed
    differently, it makes it more difficult for the reader to
    identify your prior positions.

    Not:  United States Machine Company
          Market Research Analyst, Hardware Division,
          Saginaw, Michigan

    Use something like:

    UNITED STATES MACHINE COMPANY
    Market Research Analyst, Hardware Division,
    Saginaw, Michigan                                        ____      ____

17. *Are key items highlighted* (use of indentations, capital
    letters, underlining, bold and italic type)?             ____      ____

18. *Do you have a properly produced resume?* A first-class
    printing or typing job? A conventional format? White
    paper? One side of the paper only? Properly centered?
    A lot of white space? Are you sure there are no errors in
    your spelling, grammar, and punctuation? A top-notch
    secretary can verify these for you in a few minutes.     ____      ____

19. *Have you excluded personal items that would raise
    unnecessary questions?* Your age (if over 40), divorced,
    your height and weight, a picture. Any of these items
    can cause an unfavorable reaction, and they can't really
    do anything positive for you. Incidentally, if you're

|  | | *Yes* | *No* |
|---|---|---|---|

divorced and haven't remarried, you're better off omit-
ting it or saying you're single.                                    ____   ____

20. *Have you omitted your salary?* Including it is very
    risky. While it's less so in answering ads, it's probably
    better to leave it off.                                         ____   ____

21. *Have you dated your resume?* If you have, you should
    not. You may be using your resume longer than you
    think—and the inclusion of the date simply shows how
    long you've been looking for a job.                             ____   ____

22. *Will the telephone number you list always be answered
    for you during the day?*                                        ____   ____

23. *Have you included several hobbies and community
    activities (without overemphasizing them)?* While this
    is minor, these show you as a well-rounded person.
    Often a common interest attracts attention.                     ____   ____

24. *Have you omitted mention of references?* Don't list
    your references. "References furnished on request" is
    unnecessary and amateurish. This statement is always
    implied.                                                        ____   ____

**Getting your resume critiqued**

A key step in your campaign is to get your resume properly critiqued *before* it's in final form. Remember, the best specialists will review five or six drafts, often using the opinion of several counselors within the firm. Effective criticism is particularly helpful for less-marketable individuals.

Getting good criticism isn't easy. Typical criticism is "Your resume is fine. I think I'd reword this phrase and put this third item ahead of the second. Otherwise your resume is good. You shouldn't have any trouble with it." This criticism is almost worthless because it's superficial. And it can be misleading, because you may think your resume is much better than it actually is.

If you see any critics in person, ask them to read

your resume quickly. Then ask them to describe
what their thoughts are on you as a candidate for
the job you're seeking. Ask, "If you were looking
over 25 candidates for the job I'm seeking, in what
way would you see my resume as deficient?"
Then ask:

"Is it clear what kind of a job I'm looking for?"

"Is it a reasonable objective for me?"

"What are the likely key functions of the job
I'm seeking?"

"Have I left some out?" (You might also ask
them to look over your job description.)

"Have I included some which are of minor
importance?"

"Have I given proper priority to them?"

"Have I presented each of my accomplishments
effectively?"

"Have my principal liabilities been played
down?"

Also have someone criticize your resume at his
or her leisure. This has the advantage of his being
able to give careful thought to it. If you must deliver your resume to a critic, you may want to consider doing that in person and picking it up to save
time. You do lose the give-and-take of an informal
counseling session, although you can make this up
by a subsequent phone call.

Who should review your resume for you? You
should be guided by the recommendations of
others. Evaluate their recommendations by specific
questions. Not "How was Sarah Jones as a critic?"
Rather, "What specific criticism did Sarah Jones
give you?" In the absence of favorable recommendations or professional counseling, you should seek
critics among the following:

1. Instructors and counselors at clinics, voluntary counseling services, colleges, and trade association placement offices.
2. Professional recruitment officials (employment agencies, executive recruiters, corporate personnel staffs), if they'll give it. Bear in mind their selection standards focus on highly marketable people.
3. Corporate executives.
4. Advertising people (particularly for format and wording).

Opinions on a proper resume may vary widely. Don't be surprised if they do. Use your own judgment. Use three or four critics simultaneously to speed up the process. Don't give up this criticism phase until you have a resume you're comfortable with. This is important because once you have a good resume, you'll soon be using it intensively. If you have followed these instructions carefully, your resume should be an effective one. To be sure, you may want to test market it, by mailing it to 25 percent of your target audience (see the following two chapters).

However, if it isn't providing effective entrées for you in a month or two, revise the resume. As you run across ideas for improving it, record them. Then follow the procedure outlined in this chapter again, particularly including the critiquing phase. Explaining to your chosen critics that your resume isn't working properly will stimulate their interest.

How do you determine if your resume is good enough? There's no definite answer to this question except, "Is it working?" If you have carefully followed the procedure outlined here, you should have a resume that will serve you well and be better than most of your competitors.

Should you send a revised resume to companies

which already have your first one? If your new
resume is a marked improvement and you don't
know of any active interest in you by an employer,
send your revision. You have little to lose and a lot
to gain.

Now let's see how you use a resume to approach
the visible job market.

# Chapter seven

# APPROACHING THE VISIBLE JOB MARKET

**Executive recruiters, management consultants, and CPA firms**

Who do you deal with in the visible job market? Executive recruiters, employment agencies, banks and law firms, trade associations, and college placement services. Answering employment ads is also part of this market. This chapter discusses all of them.

Executive recruiters are the most sophisticated professionals in the business. As an adjunct to their normal activities, management consultants and CPA firms perform essentially the same kind of recruiting functions. CPA firms normally are confined to only financial jobs, but many of them are becoming less active in this function. In this chapter when I refer to executive recruiters, I am referring to all three types of organizations.

All these organizations locate and screen executives for middle- and senior-management positions. They are hired and paid by the employer, who often pays a fee whether or not a recommended candidate is selected. The minimum salary of the positions that they recruit for is roughly $40,000, with a typical fee being 20 percent to 30 percent

117

of the hiree's annual compensation. As a rule of thumb, executive recruiters are looking for candidates who are earning a minimum of $1,500 per year of life. Hence a 40-year-old candidate should be earning $60,000.

What are the functions executive recruiters perform?

First, they work with top management in defining the specifications of the position the company is trying to fill. They spend considerable time with several top executives discussing the particular functions of the job, the kinds of problems that the executive will face, how the position is related to others in the company and the personality, skills, and weaknesses of some of the people who hold them. Then the company and the recruiter together draw up a comprehensive job description.

Second, executive recruiters locate and screen as many candidates as they need to be able to recommend perhaps three to five for the company's consideration. Screening usually involves several personal interviews and extensive checking of references.

A key element of an executive recruiter's skill is evaluating the chemistry of the organization and that of candidates, to see that they are as compatible as possible. The candidates recommended must have strong technical credentials and they usually represent a range of personality types and operating styles.

Finally, the recruiter works with both the company and the most favored candidates to make sure that each has a realistic understanding of the other, performing a low-key selling job on each to bring about a favorable match. Recruiters are sensitive to good matches because their long-range success depends on repeat business, which in turn only comes from a high percentage of successful assignments.

Because of this, a recruiter looks for candidates with outstanding records who are currently employed and presumably doing a first-class job. Recruiters run a greater risk than they prefer if they recommend somebody who is unemployed. If such a person is hired and doesn't work out, the employer (even though he or she made the final decision) may hold this against the recruiter in the future. Roughly only 5 percent of the candidates hired for executive-recruited jobs are unemployed. Don't, however, ignore executive recruiters in your job search.

The sources of potential candidates for assignments by recruiters are, first of all, their firm's extensive files. Recruiters are literally deluged with resumes. It is not unusual for a small recruiting firm to receive more resumes a day than the number of searches they conduct in a year. They are all reviewed and categorized so that they can be pulled out of the files on short notice. The larger firms have computerized files that include the names of up to several hundred thousand executives. Another source of candidates is a network of executives that the recruiters know of in an industry. A common technique here is for a recruiter to contact all the executives in their files from the industry or industries similar to the company for which they are conducting a search. These executives will be asked to recommend candidates for the particular assignment. Many executives are willing to make recommendations to maintain the good will of the recruiter for the future. The other source of potential executives is advertising.

A close working relationship between the recruiter and the company is important. It not only speeds up the search considerably but it also increases the likelihood of success, since the recruiter understands the organizational chemistry of the company he or she is recruiting for. So, most recruiting firms develop their own special niche (marketing, electronics, etc.).

Because of the high fees of executive recruiters, companies often won't hire them until they have exhausted all their own resources for candidates. As a result, recruiters are often given an assignment at the last minute, when the urgency of hiring somebody is great. Recruiters therefore must often work under great pressure.

Many executive job hunters spend far too much time trying to see executive recruiters, figuring that they handle the best jobs. You can usually spend your time more productively. A letter and a resume will get you enrolled in a recruiter's file, particularly if your specialty coincides with the firm's. Contacting recruiters is one instance when it is advisable to include your salary requirements. If the recruiter is searching for a candidate like yourself, you will be contacted.

Furthermore, if you are a good candidate for the kinds of jobs that the firm generally handles (even though there isn't an active search under way for such a job at the time), the recruiter will want to meet you in the future. Since recruiting is a service business, recruiters work hard to maintain the good will of their clients and potential clients. Therefore, they see a lot of individuals who are probably not good candidates for their typical assignments, although usually these are for short, courtesy interviews.

Don't expect to get a lot of advice from recruiters. Their time is limited and their orientation is toward screening candidates for specialized jobs, not advising job hunters on how to conduct a search. Recruiters are skilled in executive selection, however, and even a short interview may provide you with some good advice.

One other thought: a staff member can make a very good living conducting only 20 searches a year—which means he handles very few at one time.

Register with as many good recruiting firms in your field as possible. A list of executive recruiters showing the name, address, phone number, salary minimum, and particular area of specialty may be obtained by writing: Consultants News, Templeton Road, Fitzwilliam, New Hampshire 03447. Ask for *The Directory of Executive Recruiters.* This covers 2,300 search firms and offices in the United States, Canada, and Mexico. This firm also publishes a list of 650 search offices in 46 countries, entitled *The International Directory of Executive Recruiters.*

**Employment agencies**

Employment agencies operate in a manner similar to that of executive recruiters, but they generally handle jobs below $40,000. Employers engage them for a specific assignment, and usually but not always, the employer pays the fee. Employers often use several agencies on one search, but they pay the fee only to the agency recommending the successful candidate. Thus, these agencies can afford only a limited screening effort on each assignment. This process generally involves selecting the best candidates from the file of resumes (often without a personal interview) and forwarding them to the client. Agencies often supplement their supply of candidates by advertising.

Successful agencies run a volume business, so they are less discriminating than executive recruiters about who they see and who they recommend. Like executive recruiters, though, they also are specialists (in engineering, computers, etc.).

A letter and a resume will get you registered with an agency. Sometimes employment agencies ask you to sign a contract obligating you for the fee if the employer doesn't pay it. Be sure you know what you are signing and that you will be willing to pay the fee if you accept one of the jobs an agency handles. Fees are generally 7 percent to 12 percent of annual salary.

Executive recruiters often operate on a nationwide basis. Employment agency searches are primarily confined to one geographical area.

The best way to get information about the quality of agencies is to ask knowledgeable people in your field. Another way is by watching the employment ads in your area papers. Your best chance of seeing a key person in an agency is by appointment. If you decide to appear without appointment, do it at the least busy times—in the afternoon on any day other than Monday.

**Help wanted ads**

Answering ads is highly competitive. Frequently there will be 500 to 1,000 or more responses to one ad in *The Wall Street Journal* or in the *New York Times* Sunday edition. In spite of the poor chances of your getting an interview by answering an ad, this source is probably the best of the visible sources—if you answer ads effectively.

Because screening responses to such ads is such a tremendous undertaking, there are certain things that you can do to greatly increase your chances of getting an interview. Try to identify the company and the hiring executive. Approach him for his help, not in answer to the ad. He may be very frustrated with the delay in the hiring process and be receptive to an approach directly to him. Responses by mail are initially given a rough cut against a checklist of the highest priority items they're looking for. The most important items are usually outlined in the ad. The first step in preparing your response, then, is to carefully analyze the ad, underlining the key requirements. Then in your cover letter, if you show in one column the requirement and in the opposite column your applicable experience, you make it easy for the person doing the screening to see that you have the principal requirements (see Exhibit 7-1—the letter is a reply to the ad shown in the upper right-hand corner).

From 500 responses, the initial screening might narrow the field to 50 for more careful consideration. Because of the volume of replies, screeners have a natural bias to reject candidates—the principal reasons being too much or too little experience, or background in incompatible industries.

A more skilled screener then reviews the 50 to select perhaps 6 to 12 to interview. This second screener will probably read the resumes more carefully, although still rapidly. You may find it desirable to underline in red pencil in your resume the specific experience called for. This draws the screener's attention to your most pertinent background and should increase the chances of careful consideration.

You will spend your time best by replying to a large number of ads rather than making tailor-made responses to a few. However, for a few particularly attractive ads you may want to submit a specifically composed reply. The most practical way to do this is to have a numbered list of your PARs (Chapter Five, "Presenting Your Accomplishments"). Tell your typist to include in the cover letter the specific PARs that you want by number.

Timing your answer to the ad is important. A survey of responses to a Sunday *New York Times* ad indicated that two thirds were received the first week. One arriving within that time has little chance of being carefully examined. You have nothing to lose by submitting several answers to the ad—one right off, one a week later, and another two weeks later. The latest letter often will be screened against only a couple of others received the same day, so it will stand a better chance of careful consideration. In addition, if the early screening process fails to identify enough promis-

**EXHIBIT 7-1**

Box 5943 TIMES
The New York Times
229 W. 43rd Street
New York, New York

RE:  Industrial
      Engineer

Dear Sirs:

---

**INDUSTRIAL ENGINEER**

Leading national consumer products manufacturer located in Northwestern Connecticut is seeking a shirt-sleeve type individual to handle this position. The candidate should have a *BSIE Degree and a minimum of 5 years experience,* preferably in a *food manufacturing* environment. A thorough knowledge of *work measurement, plant layout, cost analysis, and reduction* and *methods improvement* techniques is desired. Salary commensurate with experience. Send resume including salary history and requirements in strict confidence to:

5943 TIMES

---

In answer to your ad in the May 10th Sunday Times, I think that the following highlights of my background will show that I am well qualified for the position:

| Requirement | Background |
|---|---|
| Food manufacturing | 3 years with large cosmetic manufacturer |
| Work measurement | Developed time standards for new packaging line |
| Plant layout | Assisted in redesign of layout of 100,000-square-foot plant |
| Cost analysis and reduction | Led a 3-man project team which effected a program of cost savings of $400,000 in 6 months |
| Methods improvement | Assisted in redesigning toothpaste batching operation producing 40,000 tubes per day |
| 5 years' experience | 7 years' experience |
| BSIE Degree | Rutgers BSME 1969 |

The attached resume shows other accomplishments pertinent to your Industrial Engineering job. I would like to discuss my background with you in a personal interview.

Yours very truly,

ing candidates, there may be a reluctance to review the file of rejects (on the basis, "If we couldn't find enough good candidates out of the *best* of the large number of early replies, why bother to go back through all of them again?").

The final decision to close the screening process on most executive job advertisements usually takes a month or more. Since, as we have seen, perhaps one half of *The Wall Street Journal* and *New York Times* Sunday edition ads aren't filled 90 days later, at the start of your campaign you may find it worth your while to go back and answer all the ads for your type of job that appeared in the previous 60 days.

**Banks and law firms**

There are a number of narrower entries into the visible job market, one of which is banks. Numerous large banks run an informal placement service and, of course, they tend to handle primarily financial jobs. To a lesser extent some law firms serve a similar function.

A key loan officer is your best contact to learn about bank job openings. Generally, this can be accomplished by sending a letter and a resume with your job requirements. However, if you have contacts at the bank, try to see them. Bankers who take a real interest in you can often be very helpful.

**Trade associations**

Many trade associations have a service to match open jobs and available people. Normally this service is free or available for a nominal fee, and although it is usually open to members only, you should try to register with associations in your field, even if you aren't a member. Many maintain placement services on a local chapter as well as on a national basis.

When an association's service finds a potentially good match of a candidate and a job, it usually sends the candidate's resume to the employer. The employer then takes any further action. You might, however, have the association refer any opening to you rather than referring you to the employer. This enables you to make a tailor-made presentation to the company. It is best to contact these services face to face. In addition to placement activity, some associations maintain a voluntary counseling committee which can provide a useful service.

Numerous trade organizations publish a newsletter with a section listing jobs available and available people, with brief descriptions of both. Good copy for such a situation-wanted ad is of course your advertisement, and it should show your accomplishments (not just your responsibilities), as Exhibit 7-2. There are probably only a couple of these newsletters available in your area, but they can often be a source of a few job interviews because they may have a large mailing list.

**EXHIBIT 7-2**

Engineering Executive

Chief Engineer, $25 million company, staff of 27, 23 years experience with three companies in tool design and engineering of new products in the electronics field. Upgraded staff in tight labor market; rapid, low-cost, and successful development of new products; helped increase sales by improving communications of engineering and sales personnel.

BSME Carnegie Tech.

**College alumni placement services**

Many alumni placement services—college, fraternity, and sorority—have expanded considerably because of the increased demands for them. Most of them are geared to graduating students, but some provide these same kinds of services to alumni, though usually to the younger and highly marketable. Services vary but they usually include an available job-matching program as well as limited counseling services, often at a modest fee. These services invariably have access to vocational-counseling services and sometimes know of good professional job counselors or psychologists. They sometimes have a good resource library of information on companies and industries. Some college career counseling services provide a monthly newsletter listing available people. You should register for this service.

If you no longer live near your college, try other good college placement services in your area. Often they will talk to you and sometimes accept you on their rolls. Such college services are among the few services that work primarily for a job seeker. Therefore they are quite knowledgeable about local market conditions and available resources.

**Personnel executives**

If you are seeking a senior management position, personnel executives ordinarily are of very limited use unless you know one personally. If you are seeking a lower-level position, they may be of some use—but most personnel executives' basic responsibility in hiring is to fill the job requisitions sent to them. Only rarely do they try to find a job for somebody within the organization, unless the candidate is in the elite. Because of this, if you are making a blind prospecting contact with a company, it should be to a line executive, not to personnel.

Personnel executives, however, because of their skills in evaluating people, frequently take an important part in the process of screening executive job candidates. And they may have veto power over hiring.

Because the visible market is the source of such a large number of good jobs and it is so easy to make a wide variety of contacts there, you can easily find yourself devoting far more time to it than is warranted. Unless you have a really outstanding record, spend no more than a quarter of your time approaching it. Let's now see how you might deal with the more promising hidden job market.

# Chapter eight

# APPROACHING THE HIDDEN JOB MARKET

**Hidden jobs**    I said earlier that the hidden market handles about 75 percent of all available jobs. That figure might surprise you, but research and my own experience bear it out.

The hidden market contains jobs that will open owing to retirement, someone leaving, understaffing, or expansion, but for which no provision has yet been made. Mostly though, that market holds positions of which employers are not consciously aware. In the majority of cases, it is up to the job hunter to stimulate a recognition of need, then to show how he or she can fulfill it.

Essentially, you uncover the hidden job market by planting in an employer's mind the idea that *you* can make a difference to a company. *You* have the skills needed to solve a problem, experience in expanding business, ideas on how to cut costs, and so on.

Selling yourself here is different from selling yourself in the visible job market. There the employer recognizes a need and the job description is the center of attention, the measuring stick against which you are initially screened. Compromising here and there usually follows, but the successful candidate will be the one who fits the job description in most respects.

No such recognition of need exists in the hidden market and, of course, neither does any such obvious means of measurement as a job description— at least in the beginning. You must stimulate an employer to realize how you can contribute to fulfilling his or her basic need—the need for continued success in business and company growth. This may seem like a tough selling job—and it can be—but it can also bring a rich reward: a job you like and one in which you'll be successful.

In the hidden job market, *you* are the center of attention, and the measuring stick. Once an employer recognizes your value, he or she will next consider how things might be arranged, or rearranged, to take advantage of it. Richard D. Gleason, founder of the outplacement firm, Man Marketing Services, Inc., of Chicago describes the process in this way: "We teach the executive to look for a problem for which his skills are the solution."

How do you tap the hidden job market? That's what this chapter is about.

**Developing your list of contacts**

Your contacts, especially the influential ones, can be of great value if used effectively. So your first step is to prepare your list of contacts and key executives. *Contacts* are people you know or have been referred to and who you will want to touch for advice, job leads, job-hunting tips, referrals, and so on. You can identify these people with a little effort (company and bank officers, trade association executives, executive recruiters, etc.).

*Key executives* are people who are in a position to hire you. Your objective is to see as many of them as possible. To develop a list of key executives, you must first identify their companies and then find the proper individual to see within each. Always approach any organization through a specific individual. Because presidents have been so deluged by job seekers, and depending on the level of position you're seeking, address your approach to a lower-level executive, such as the executive vice president or the functional head of your field of expertise (e.g., marketing vice president, general sales manager). Aim for a person no more than two levels above the job you're shooting for.

"I don't have any contacts" is a common complaint. But is that really so? Here are some thoughts on the type of people to include on your list: friends, relatives, professional men (doctors, lawyers, accountants), ministers, businessmen (bankers, consultants, insurance agents, stockbrokers, company executives), past employers, former associates, competitors, salespeople, suppliers, customers, professors, politicians, fundraisers, members and officials of civic organizations.

To develop your preliminary lists of contacts, search your personal address and phone books, your business phone and address list, your gift lists, your alumni directory, your business directories, your trade association membership lists, your club membership list, and so on. In addition to people you know, include people you can probably get an introduction to easily. You may be embarrassed to call on your most influential contacts. That's a natural feeling. But they may be the people who can provide you with the best referrals—and they may surprise you with their positive response. You have nothing to lose—but they probably won't seek you out. Don't underestimate your contacts. Often people you wouldn't expect to, have very influential relationships with key people.

"I don't want to use my friends," is another reaction you may have. Does this really make sense with all you have at stake? Turn the situation around: Would many of these friends ask for your help if they thought you might be able to assist them? Of course, they would.

The names of key executives can be developed directly from: Dun & Bradstreet, *Million Dollar Directory* (companies with a net worth of more than $1 million, or *Middle Market Directory* (companies with a net worth between $500,000 to $1 million), regional directories (e.g., *New England Directory of Manufacturers*), or *Moody's Industrial Manual.* The names of companies (without the names of the executives) can be developed from state industrial directories, *Fortune First* and *Second 500* lists, directories of particular industries (publishers, banks, and so on), chamber of commerce lists, the Yellow Pages of the phone book. One of the best sources may be a trade-association membership list. Another particularly useful one is a list of your fellow college alumni in the area. In addition to company and title, you can learn the home address, directorships, college, and so on of many executives from Standard and Poor's *Register of Corporations, Directors and Executives.* A good business library will have most of these directories available—and often can be helpful in providing other such sources. Placement offices of colleges can also be helpful in this research work. In developing your list put particular emphasis on your present industry, a secondary emphasis on related industries. But be careful: a recent survey showed that names, addresses, and titles of about one third of the executives on a mailing list prepared from directories were wrong. So verify your top-priority names and addresses by phone.

In pulling your list of contacts together, include the name and address of the company and the name and title of the specific key executive you want to contact. Where it is available, it is also helpful to include key general information about the company such as a list of its products, its sales volume, and the number of employees.

Additional ways to explore for contacts and key executives are as follows:

1. Your best bet is to get three referrals from every contact and every key executive, even those who are not interested in hiring you.

2. Try to get referrals to companies in which there have been major executive changes within a year (particularly from someone brought in from the outside in your particular function). Other companies that are likely to need key people are those undergoing major changes (those acquiring other companies or recently bought out, those introducing new products or announcing new contracts, and those undergoing major financing or plant expansions). As you see your contacts and key executives, use this as a checklist to jog their memories for referrals.

3. People who have been recently hired (as announced in the newspapers) for a job similar to the one you're seeking may have had several offers. An offer that was of no interest to them might be to you. Ask recruiters, employment agencies, bankers, etc., who has found a job in your field lately.

4. Try to keep in touch with others who are going through a job search now; you may know of jobs that may be helpful to them, and they to you.

5. Companies that are expanding are obvious. Companies in trouble may offer opportunities also, but be realistic about the risks involved.

6. Circulate socially as well as at your trade association, church, community meetings, and so

on. This is no time to go into hiding. Contacts made in improbable places sometimes prove to be very valuable.

7. If you ride the train, sit with a different acquaintance every day, and tell him or her what you are looking for.

8. If you belong to a national association (for example, Financial Executives Institute), send your resume to their placement people in other areas, not just the local one.

9. Read what business and community leaders in your area are saying; maybe their ideas can mean an opportunity for you. Reference to a particular speech may be an excellent way to get an entrée.

10. See or call all the people you know who have been through a successful job campaign in recent years. Ask about who was useful to them, techniques that were particularly helpful, and so on.

Now that you have an extensive list of contacts and key executives, prepare a 3x5 card for each company. This card will then become a record of your progress with the contact. Arrange your list of contacts and key executives in priority order.

**EXAMPLE 8-1**
Company card

Thomas J. Brown, VP Engineering      743-982-7953
XYZ Company
147 Elm St., Peoria, IL  56392

Precision lathes. Sales 35,000,000. Employees 975.

Secretary:  Jane Smith
Referral:   Jack Thomas
7/9/76      Mailed referral letter.
7/12/76     Phoned: Appointment 7/18.
7/18/76     No job available. Referral: Dave Sawyer—Lillian Morrison.

Approach your top-priority key executives by the referral method; the lower priority people by a telephone interview or other methods described later.

Two final thoughts: Contacts can be extremely useful and you should use them—but don't use them as a crutch. It may turn out that you can use your time more effectively on other methods of getting actual interviews. While contacts are important, they aren't essential. You can have many, but if you don't make a favorable impression, they will be of limited use. On the other hand, if you're an effective job hunter, you can develop all the useful contacts you'll need.

## Referrals

*Initial contact*

On your list of contacts will be the names of some people you feel will be most able to help you. Ask their help especially to obtain interviews with key executives. This is the technique most highly recommended by outplacement counselors. In brief interviews plumb your best contacts for any thoughts they may have about job possibilities and advice on your campaign, and then ask for referrals to other key executives. These referrals enable you to see a great many executives who may be in a position to hire you. If, when you see them, no specific prospect for a job in their own organization occurs, encourage them to provide you with referrals to still other key people. Obviously, the more impressed these individuals are with your presentation and background, the greater the chance they will find a position for you in their organization or refer you to other top individuals.

You might approach executives to whom you have been referred by phone; otherwise approach them by letter with a follow-up phone call. In either case, once you have an appointment, mail them a resume so they can quickly familiarize themselves with your background before you see them. A typical prospecting letter on a referral campaign might be:

Mr. Walter Wilson, Treasurer
Ace Products Inc.
37 Wilson Street
Birmingham, AL

Dear Mr. Wilson:

Your reputation in the field of semiconductors has prompted me to seek your advice. I am presently facing an important decision on my career. I am writing to you particularly because I am looking for a very special kind of situation.

My objective and an analysis of my background are included in the enclosed resume. I realize that there is little chance of your having a suitable position for me in your company.

However, I would very much like to hear your thoughts on how I should conduct my campaign. Perhaps you would give me 10 to 15 minutes of your time to discuss this matter.

Early next week I will call you to see if we can arrange a mutually convenient meeting.

Sincerely,

Note the following five features of this letter.

1. Personalize the opening as much as possible.
2. Ask for help—not a job.
3. Ask for a personal interview—and stipulate that it will be for only a few minutes.
4. Clearly state that you recognize there is little chance of a suitable job for you in the organization at this time.
5. Control the follow-up by stating that you will phone for an appointment.

Make the letter as personal as possible. Its content will vary, depending on such things as how

well you know the addressee (if at all), whether
you're seeking a job now (or in the future), and
whether you're seeking an interview or merely
writing for information.

Alternative openings:

> Ms. Sylvia Fowler of Ultimate Investments, Inc.,
> has suggested I write to you.

> Since you are a fellow alumnus of Hamilton who
> has achieved success in business, I am writing
> you on a matter of personal importance.

> It's been six months since I ran into you at the
> Electronics Convention in Chicago.

Here are several ideas to make responses to your
letter more favorable. Mail received on days other
than Monday or Friday is likely to get more attention. If your letter is marked *Confidential,* it is
more likely to get your addressee's attention.
Monarch stationery (7 inches x 10 inches) appears
more personal and therefore may be more eye-
catching. Stipulate that you will follow-up with a
phone call, because invariably only a small percentage of these people will contact you.

Since this technique is being used more and
more, the demands on key executives for such
interviews have increased greatly. Often, even with
referral by a key person to a close friend, you may
meet resistance. In these cases consider the following approaches.

*The*
*follow-up*

The way you handle your call for an appointment is all important. A call to someone you don't
know can easily get a negative response—unless you
are well prepared. Prepare an outline of what you
plan to say, and rehearse it. With skillful handling
you should be able to get interviews perhaps 75
percent of the time.

Your first hurdle will probably be the key execu-

tive's secretary. Use a firm, positive approach and
call the secretary if possible by name. Be prepared
for her "closing the door" on you. Emphasize
you're not approaching the executive for a job—
just for a few minutes for his help. Try calling
before or after regular hours, at lunch time or on
Saturday, when the secretary won't be there.

When you are connected with the executive, try
to get an interview. "Mr. Wilson, I wrote to you
recently to ask for a 10-minute meeting to get your
advice on a matter of great importance to me. My
resume indicated my 15 years of sales management
experience, the most recent 3 years as sales manager of XYZ Company. I am not asking for a job,
but your experience in the electronics business
could be very helpful in the decision I have to make
now. When would it be convenient for you to see
me?"

Be prepared for negative responses such as "too
busy," "leaving town for a week," "no current
openings," and so on. Be ready with a reply to
overcome these objections and then emphasize
again your need to get information. Repeat that
you're not looking for a job—only advice.

"Would Tuesday at 9:45 be convenient?" (Note
this time implies a meeting of only 15 minutes,
whereas 9:30 indicates at least a half-hour meeting,
and 10:00 perhaps an hour.) If you are turned
down for an interview, try to get as much help as
you can in the phone conversation. "Could you
suggest any companies that I should see?" If a
company is named, ask whom he suggests you see
there. If he is unresponsive, you should use several
joggers, like "Can you think of any company that
might need a financial executive with strong experience in cost reduction and developing reporting
systems?" Or "Would you think there might be a
need at Acme Machine Tools? or Davis Steel? or
Banner Electronics?" Your goal should be to get
three referrals from each interview.

You may then approach any names that person gives you by saying, "Mr. Simpson of Ace Products thought it would be useful to see you."

This procedure of phoning for an appointment emphasizes the need to improve your effectiveness on the telephone (i.e., in getting through to the person you want to talk to, in developing his or her interest, in getting interviews, and in getting information). Take five minutes after each call to record what transpired and ask yourself: "If I knew beforehand what I know now, what would I have done differently?"

*Interview strategy*

In a referral interview, your strategy has to be flexible because you probably will have little idea ahead of time why the key executive is willing to see you. In a small fraction of these interviews that person may indicate that he or she is considering you for an opening. If this is the case, use the technique of the three-stage interview (described later) in which you try to get the key executive to reveal the problems he or she is concerned about in your field before you try to make an impression with your background. In most referral interviews, however, there's only a slight chance of a job; therefore plan your approach to get as much help from this key executive as possible.

A personal interview usually will start off with your being asked to outline what you are looking for and what your credentials are for such a job. You should have a well-organized presentation which will cover your overall background including one or two examples of experience that an employer would be looking for in the kind of job you are seeking. This presentation should be consolidated into two or three minutes. Your initial presentation may well get a specific response from the interviewer asking for more information on something you've mentioned. If not, the interviewer probably is indicating that he or she wants you to carry the ball further. It is now appropriate to ask whether the interviewer would like to hear more about type of experience X or Y. The response to this provides you with some direction on what he or she may be interested in. As the conversation develops, it may take the direction of one or more problems that are of particular concern to the interviewer. Be prepared to ask one or two questions concerning these particular items, stressing the fact that you have expertise in solving some of the kinds of problems he or she may be having.

This is your interview with key executive Betty Brown, district manager of ABC Electronics.

It may well be that she clearly discourages you from relating any of your experience to her particular problem. In such an event, you might ask her some specific questions such as:

"If you were looking for someone in my field of expertise, what would be the most important requirements of the job?"

"Can you think of any important functional experience I'm missing?"

"Have I mentioned experience that you feel is irrelevant or over-emphasized?"

"In____(a key function previously mentioned by interviewer), what depth of experience would you be looking for?"

Continue by outlining how you're going about your campaign and asking for her reaction to it. Finally, ask her for her ideas on people you should see. Some of these may be in the employment field and others may be key executives. It is great if she volunteers to arrange an introduction by phone or letter for you, but don't count on it. She may not give you any names at all, but your objective should be to get at least three referrals to key executives. If she will provide you with names, they will probably be on a level comparable to hers. The more favorable impression you make, the better referrals you will get. If she will not give you such names voluntarily, bring up the names of a couple of companies that you might be interested in. "Would you think it would be a good idea if I saw somebody at the XYZ Company or M&M Machine Company?" She will probably say yes, and she might suggest several other companies that you ought to see. Then ask if she knows who would be the best person for you to see at each of these companies. If she does not volunteer to contact them or say that you can use her name, ask her if you may. Such an interview may last only 10 minutes, but it may last an hour or more.

To get the most help from key executives who have given you referrals, make sure you inform them of what transpired with each person they referred you to. And always send a brief thank-you note, even if it is handwritten. But don't let the matter rest here—phone each referral in a month or six weeks to see if he or she has any more ideas.

There undoubtedly will be some companies that you would like to approach directly, but to which you have no specific entrée. You can still use this technique of "asking for help, and not a job" by making a *blind contact* (one for which you have no referral) with a specific executive. Done skillfully you should be able to get a blind-contact interview perhaps half the time.

**Telephone prospecting**

Another direct approach employs telephone interviews. This method is similar to the referral method, although there are certain key differences. In the first place, only a few calls result in a personal interview, a prime objective of hidden-market approaches. This is offset by the great increase in the number of opportunities to get the ideas of key executives. Furthermore, the result of the vast majority of referral interviews is information which may be useful for your campaign and additional referrals, and these results can often be accomplished as effectively on the phone. This technique hasn't been used a lot for senior management jobs, but it can be useful, if handled skillfully. Often a call will take only five minutes, and a volume of 10 calls a day to key executives should develop several interviews in a week. A letter such as the following will provide an entrée that will result in considerably better results than a completely cold call.

May 26, 1978

Mr. James Belknap
Executive Vice President
Franklin Motors Company
160 Collidge Avenue
Norfolk, VA

Dear Mr. Belknap:

Currently I'm planning to make an important career step. I'm looking for an opportunity to apply my talents as a marketing executive of a growing business.

My purpose and accomplishments are summarized on the enclosed resume. My University of Illinois accounting degree combined with hands-on experience as Assistant Marketing Manager of M&N Steel Company have given me broad exposure to the business world. I have developed a strong and broad range of marketing and administrative skills. My accomplishments speak for my ability to handle complex or delicate responsibilities.

I would appreciate any advice or references you may have. I'll call shortly to chat on the phone for a few minutes.

Sincerely yours,

Theodore N. Bronson

Enclosure

Preparation for your phone call in solicitation is more important than in the referral method. Here again you must be ready to handle possible obstruction from the executive's secretary. Your method of dealing with this is similar to the referral method discussed above. Suppose, though, Mr. Belknap's secretary states: "I remember you. You want a personal interview." Reply: "No, that is not true. Actually all I'm asking for is a few minutes of Mr. Belknap's time on the phone."

Here the objective of your phone call is not to get a *help* interview, rather it is to get an on-the-phone job interview, and failing this, to get as much help as you can. Therefore, this is much more of a selling type of phone call than is used in the referral method. Furthermore, Mr. Belknap will only vaguely remember your letter and resume, and he may try to find it, which will divert attention from your sales presentation. So use a telegraphic presentation to put him at ease by assuring him that you are going to quickly tell him what he needs to know. This will make him more receptive to what you are trying to get across.

To improve the effectiveness of your presentation, develop an introductory script. Your message should take no longer than one or two minutes to relate. Polish it until it is concise and tells your key highlights. Recording it is useful, particularly if you can get someone to listen to it critically. Taping some actual calls can be easily done also, with good criticism of your telephone effectiveness being particularly helpful. Sound positive, but natural. Talk up and directly into the phone. Standing up when you are making your phone call often can make you sound more sure of yourself. Practice the script until you are comfortable with it. Your script might take form as follows:

| *Purpose* | *The detailed script* |
|---|---|
| Your objective. | Hello, this is Ted Bronson. You may recall I sent you my resume and a letter a few days ago in which I explained that I'm looking for a position as a <u>marketing executive.</u> |
| Your background. | My educational background at the <u>University of Illinois</u> with a Business <u>Management</u> degree and my experience as <u>Assistant Marketing Manager</u> of M&N Steel Company give me strong experience. |
| A cue to stimulate his thinking. | Now I'm looking to broaden my responsibilities. I'm looking for the <u>names of firms</u> that might be able to use my skills. |
| | You may recall my areas of strength make me a businessman's <u>marketing man,</u> a sales <u>problem solver.</u> |
| Cues and accomplishments (they're key to getting interviews). | For example, I developed new uses that realized $3,500,000 of sales annually.<br>I reorganized the Philadelphia region increasing sales 28% in two years.<br>So I'm wondering if you know of any situations which might: |
| Additional cues. | 1. Have <u>growing pains</u> and need someone to take over some of the <u>marketing functions.</u><br>2. Have <u>sales troubles</u> and need them addressed by a <u>problem solver.</u><br>3. <u>Need a financially-oriented marketing person.</u> |
| More cues. | Perhaps you know of people who might know of these types of situations such as a <u>banker, a lawyer, a consultant?</u> |

The use of a detailed script can be especially helpful for the first dozen or so calls. Then you'll find that you only need to refer to the key words (those that are underlined). You may find it useful to list them in the column where the "Purpose" notes are shown in this example.

This telephone interviewing procedure allows you to cover a lot of companies in a short time. It is particularly useful when you have run out of contacts and direct referrals.

A recommended telephone campaign, using batches of 50 companies a week, consists of the following sequence:

| Week | Activity |
|---|---|
| 1 . . . . . . . | Making a list of the companies, key executives, etc. |
| 2 . . . . . . . | Preparing and mailing the letters to them |
| 3 . . . . . . . | Phoning for appointments |
| 4 . . . . . . . | Interviews |

In the fourth week, you are researching your fourth batch, you're mailing your third, you're phoning your second, and having job interviews with your first. By the 8th to 10th week you're also phoning back to your first batch. This method should produce something like 2 percent job interviews if done effectively.

Either the referral method or the telephone-interview method is particularly effective if you have a really good mailing list. If for example you are at a lower level, a mailing list for marketing executives of the local chapter of the American Marketing Association would be invaluable.

**Interviews for information**

This is a variation of the referral method, but it is strictly an approach asking for specific information. It is particularly appropriate when you are making your survey of various types of careers you may want to pursue. It is also appropriate for someone who is just starting out or at the junior-executive level, or is thinking of changing careers. As in the referral method, use an approach by either letter (stipulating that you will call for an appointment) or directly by phone.

If you are approaching top management people, you probably stand a better chance of success making your approach by letter. With the right technique you ought to be able to get in to see almost everybody you contact. A typical approach by phone might be: "I have called you because of your many years of experience in the brokerage business. That business attracts me, and I would like to talk to you about the opportunities in it, and how well my qualifications would fit. I realize that you probably don't have a job available, and I really am not looking for one at this time, as I am making a survey of possibilities in this industry as compared to a couple of other types of jobs." When you have decided on your career objective, go back to each of your contacts in that field and state that you would like their help in locating a job.

**The broadcast letter**

The broadcast letter is an alternative to the telephone-interview approach. This method was perfected by Carl Boll and is detailed in his book *Executive Jobs Unlimited* (New York: Macmillan, 1979). It consists of a mass mailing of a specialized hard sell letter to the president of a great many companies (50 to 100 a week). The one-page letter stresses only your specific accomplishments, which are outlined using numbers of dollars saved, sales increased, numbers of employees supervised, and so on. You do not specify where this experience was gained, since if your experience was in electronics, a chemical company might discount much of it. If you have reasonable experience and spell it out effectively, you arouse interest in employers to consider you, often to fill a need unrecognized at the time.

Although this technique was very effective in the job-hunter's market when it was written in 1965, because of the employer's job market since that time and the fact that this technique has been overused, it has become less so. It shouldn't be overlooked, however, and should be used after two or three months in your campaign if other means are not producing good results.

Now, a positive response probably occurs in perhaps only 1 percent or 2 percent of a mailing, but occasionally it will run as high as 5 percent. There are two variations on the technique which increase the rate of favorable response considerably. First, as in other contacts, mail your letter to the executive two levels (or even one level) above the kind of job you're looking for. Second, stipulate that you will phone for an appointment. You should make a mailing every week to perhaps 100 or more companies. Experience shows that a mailing to the same list two months later may produce about the same result, because there is a constant turnover in management's personnel needs. There is no point at all in making such a mailing unless the letter is extremely good.

Note that the letter does not include a resume. Including a resume greatly reduces the percentage of response because it spells out too many details that may raise questions in the mind of an employer. In fact, do not take your resume to any interview you get using this method. Instead, after an interview make up a tailor-made resume which you can include with your thank-you letter.

Sophisticated employers (i.e., the larger companies) and employment professionals are usually very critical of broadcast letters. The best markets for them are small- and medium-sized companies, service organizations, and nonprofit organizations.

EXAMPLE 8-2
A broadcast letter

Mr. Melvin Babson, Vice President
Ohio Products Inc.
47 Norwalk St.
Cleveland, OH 23472

Dear Mr. Babson:

If you are not fully satisfied with results being generated by your company's sales and marketing efforts, I'd like to talk with you about the possibility of joining your management team to help remedy that situation.

Among my achievements as sales manager and then sales and marketing vice president are:

Since 1976, increased annual sales almost 40% (sales up $8 million) with 1980 profits up $980,000 over 1976.

Marketed new technical and nontechnical products. They made up 38% of 1980 sales.

Freed working capital by narrowing product line and developing new inventory controls (8% fewer $ in finished goods year-end 1980 versus 1976 even though sales up almost 40%!).

Entered new markets (over $1.8 million sales 1980).

These advances, the result of carefully-made plans and team effort, were hammered out in a declining industry at the expense of entrenched active competitors. This was accomplished without price cutting and, in several instances, with new premium-priced products.

Before writing to you, Mr. Babson, I've gathered information about your company. I believe you will find my experience and background most compatible with your situation.

If you feel there is a possibility of mutual interest, I'd welcome the opportunity to explore it with you in a meeting at your convenience.

Sincerely,

Frank M. Brown

EXAMPLE 8-2 *(continued)*

Background data: Over 16 years with present company which I joined as salesman, becoming sales manager in 1970, vice president in 1976, 44 years old, in excellent health, married with 3 children, M.B.A. from New York University Business School and A.B. Haverford College.

**A mailing to friends**

One of the keys to a successful campaign is using your time and efforts wisely, so setting priorities is important. You will undoubtedly have a few friends and contacts who are in influential positions, and who you might try to interview early in your campaign. Other friends, although undoubtedly a lot of them are interested in helping you, are not in such influential positions. The majority of them will be willing to see you and to refer you to people like themselves. But by seeing many of them at the beginning, you can find yourself on a merry-go-round of interviews with little chance of success. A mass mailing to these less-influential contacts asking for their help and for specific ideas is probably the most efficient way to contact them. Out of a large group there may be a few that will come up with specific ideas that could be of great help. Stating in the letter that you will probably want to see them when your campaign gets going allows you to respond to any ideas that sound promising and leaves the door open for you to set up personal interviews later. Include a resume with the letter; most of them know that you were sales manager of Gardner Electronics, for example, but they probably don't know anything about your specific responsibilities and your record there. An example of such a letter is shown on the next page.

Where practical, use a modification of the letter to request an interview or to arrange for a phone call.

EXAMPLE 8-3

Mr. Edward Dickson, Vice President
Folger Manufacturing Company
492 Chestnut Street
Pittsburgh, PA

Dear Ed:

Recent cutbacks in the aerospace industry have resulted
in the elimination of the department at XYZ where I have
been for 10 years. While I have several situations pending
still within the company, none of them appear to have the
future possibilities I would like. With the company's help
I am just starting to pursue outside opportunities as a
possible alternative.

I am writing to you for your help. I wouldn't expect
that you would know of anything suitable, but I want you
to know of my availability. The attached resume will give
you more details of my background. Would you let me
know if you have any thoughts that would be helpful on
my campaign? Perhaps you might suggest several people it
would be useful for me to see.

If I find I am coming to Pittsburgh, I will let you know
in advance—so I might stop in for a brief chat at your
convenience.

Sincerely,

**Situation
wanted ads**

This approach used carelessly can be expensive
and fruitless. Used judiciously, however, it may be
a productive source of a few leads. Undoubtedly
you will be deluged by a lot of junk mail from such
an ad, but this is irrelevant if you get one or two
good leads. Probably the best source for success of
such ads is trade-association journals. A former vice
president of a $800 million company got the lead
for an excellent job five miles from his home by
placing an ad in *The Wall Street Journal.* Ad space
in the newspapers with the best chances of yielding

you success is expensive and should be used on a limited basis. These are *The Wall Street Journal,* the *New York Times* Sunday edition, and metropolitan newspapers' Sunday editions. If you use the ad technique, emphasize accomplishments (see the ad in Exhibit 7-2).

**Additional thoughts**

1. Although there are numerous exceptions, as a career progresses there is a distinct overall trend in job changes to lower-quality (i.e., less well-established and higher-risk) companies. An aggressive and imaginative campaign can greatly improve your chances of getting a good job with a high-quality company.

2. Take every job interview you're offered, even though some may be for jobs you don't think you'd like. You never know what useful information you'll gather. Sometimes jobs are changed to make them more attractive. Finally, getting an offer may allow you to spring loose another job you're really interested in.

3. Be flexible—don't commit yourself entirely to one technique until you are satisfied that it is working. Try several techniques and test them.

4. Work on your telephone technique. This is something that you may have to develop skill in. Beginning insurance salespeople are urged to practice it a lot. Some effort on this score can improve your technique considerably. While you may have used the phone a lot on your job in the past, you probably haven't done a lot of selling of yourself on it.

5. If you are called for an interview involving large travel expenses, get a clear understanding ahead of time on who will pay for the trip.

6. Try taking executive recruiters and employment agency people to lunch. They have to eat, and getting to know you as a person may

stimulate them to make a special effort for
you.

7.  Visit employment-center cities near you—you
    open up a large market in this way, and often
    can get additional ideas.

8.  Hiring activities are seasonal so gear your
    efforts accordingly. A mass mailing two weeks
    before Christmas probably will be pretty in-
    effective. Hiring drags in the summer also be-
    cause vacations slow down the process of
    seeing the necessary people.

9.  Have a secretary place phone calls for inter-
    views, if possible: "Mr. Smith of XYZ is call-
    ing Mr. Jones." If you get turned down by an
    executive's secretary, you may want to try to
    make a direct contact at off hours when it is
    much more likely that an executive will
    answer his or her own phone.

10. In a blind-mailing experiment, try using a
    blank envelope marked "Personal and Confi-
    dential." Perhaps try a special delivery letter
    or a telegram with a letter to follow.

11. Periodically review whether or not you are
    getting interviews with *people who could
    really hire you.* If not, review your approach.

12. Don't limit your search to your area—even if
    you do not want to move. Good offers else-
    where can perhaps be used to spring an offer
    loose in your area, or make you realize other
    areas may be just as good for you profession-
    ally and as good for your family as your cur-
    rent one.

13. Follow up every few weeks with the best con-
    tacts (those with the best ideas, the most in-
    fluential). They are constantly seeing poten-
    tial employees and other job hunters—make
    sure they keep you in mind. They'll tell you
    if you are a nuisance. A note indicating prog-

ress on a matter you discussed is a good way of keeping in touch.

14. Keep a notebook with you at all times. Add to your list every name you come across. Keep doing it until you accept your new job.

The approaches to the visible and hidden job markets cited in this and the preceding chapter, if carried out effectively and aggressively, should result in a fair number of job interviews. To make the most of them, you should do a good job on the next step, Preparing for Interviews.

# Chapter nine

# PREPARING FOR INTERVIEWS

In previous chapters and especially in Chapter Eight we've discussed some aspects of interviews. Interviewing plays such an important role in executive job hunting that in this chapter I want to share with you some tips on how to prepare yourself.

At this stage it doesn't matter whether its for an actual job in the visible market or for prospecting in the hidden market. It doesn't matter where or how you got your lead or referral. You have an appointment for an interview. And you want to be ready for it.

The first thing you want to do—in any interview —is to put your best foot forward when you tell who you are and explain what you have to offer. This means preparation for remember, you'll probably have no more than an hour to sell yourself.

**Presenting your background**

For years executives have been asking applicants questions, yet they often fail to prepare themselves for interviews when they find themselves on the other side of the desk. The importance of presenting yourself effectively in an interview has already been shown by Bill Jackson's experience (see "I Really Don't Have Many Accomplishments" in Chapter Five).

Fortunately, presenting your background in an interview is essentially extending your resume. So, much of your homework is already done; the accomplishments and skills that you are going to be talking about will already have been developed in the preparation of your resume.

You cannot expect your accomplishments to speak entirely for themselves. Bragging, on the other hand, can just as surely turn the interviewer off. Get in between.

Some people are more facile in presenting themselves than others. They embellish each accomplishment and make it sound great. Many other people are ineffective in interviews because they do exactly the opposite. They may have been conditioned all their lives not to talk about themselves. Sometimes this is why they are looking for a job in the first place. If you are among the many who are not effective in selling themselves, you've got to change. Fortunately, with good preparation, careful strategy and some practice, you should be able to improve your skill in selling yourself. You will have gone a long way toward overcoming this difficulty once you have prepared a complete list of your accomplishments and developed your PARs to help you present most favorably what you've done. To get the maximum mileage out of your PARs, be sure that you analyze each one or each part of it to show the variety of skills involved. For example, if you developed a new system, you can use this fact to show your problem-solving ability, your effectiveness in selling ideas and winning cooperation, and your ability to work under pressure and deliver what's needed on time. A useful way of having your PARs at your fingertips in an interview is to write them on 3 x 5 cards and memorize them.

Thorough preparation is the first step in overcoming the "third degree" atmosphere job hunters often find themselves in during an interview.

**Typical questions**

Ninety percent of the questions you will be asked can be predicted and prepared for. Jot them down—and prepare answers to particularly sensitive ones. First, outline on paper what you are going to say. Second, prepare a 3 x 5 card for each answer, which you can use for practice in the same way as for your PARs. Familiarize yourself with these answers but don't try to memorize them verbatim. In answering a question be clear, concise, and positive. One to two minutes ordinarily should be enough.

In answering questions:

1. Listen to the question. Be sure you understand it. Ask for clarification if necessary. Occasionally repeating the question shows you're really listening.
2. Take enough time to think through your answer.
3. Use only positive information if possible. Be complete enough, but try not to open areas of difficulty. Be truthful.
4. Preparation of your answers to typical questions often can enable you to turn what might be an awkward question to your advantage.

Two ways of answering particularly sensitive questions—restating the question and the three-tier answer—can be useful. You can see how the first strategy works for the question, "Why were you fired?" By restating the question, for example, "Why did I leave XYZ?" you've given yourself some additional time to organize your answer, you have not admitted to having been fired, and you have given yourself more latitude in the way you can phrase the answer. Most interviewers will not recognize what you have done.

You may want to prepare sequentially staged or multitiered answers for the difficult questions, for example, "Why did you leave XYZ?" The first-tier answer gives the most acceptable interpretation of events possible, such as, "I was ready to move on to a new position," or, "When Jack Smith took over as sales manager, four of his seven department heads left within a year." Stop, and do not go on unless the interviewer demands more information. If he or she does, you might then say, "There was a philosophical difference between my boss and me as to where we were trying to take the operation," or "There was a great deal of turmoil after Jack Smith arrived. What had been a good atmosphere producing good results turned into a jungle." But that's only if you're asked for a second-tier answer. (Most interviewers won't pursue the line of questioning a second time—they are usually satisfied with the first-tier answer.) Hold the third tier in abeyance until asked directly; then your answer might be something like, "I was fired, because he wanted his own man."

Receiving responses in stages leads interviewers to feel that they have been answered and they have to ask for more if they desire it. This helps an applicant who is nervous about having left a previous job under a cloud to know that he or she has a carefully prepared answer which will defuse the issue. After you answer each question, try to redirect the conversation by asking another question, for example, "We were talking earlier about sales training, would you like to hear more about that or how we were able to increase sales by 35 percent in two years?" Asking a question in this way directs the interviewer to choose a subject involving a problem of interest to him or her. Or perhaps, "Many people feel I'm too results-oriented. I've always prided myself on being able to get a lot done." If the implication is that you're overly aggressive, you might want to add, "But I've always been able to get things done and maintain a good relationship with those I work with."

Here are some alternate strategies for answering difficult questions:

1. Answer the question with another question. "Aren't you overqualified?" "What makes you think I'm overqualified?"

2. Take the offensive in your answer by turning an apparent liability into an asset. "Why didn't you go to college?" A good answer might be, "I am self-educated. I have competed continuously with college-educated people and have won out." Or if an employer asks, "What is your greatest weakness?" a good answer might be, "Some people say I'm a workaholic."

3. Acknowledge the statement and then rebut it (for example, the "yes, but . . . ." answer). "It's true, I don't have machine-tool industry experience, but I didn't have metal-fabricating experience before I went to XYZ. In a matter of six months, I was able to straighten out a messed-up computer operation." A second-tier answer might be "Didn't Bill Farlow come from the steel business and Virginia Wheeler from a rubber company?"

4. "I don't know," may be the best answer you can give to certain questions.

5. If you are asked a new key question in an interview, add it to your list and prepare an answer for it.

6. Develop a strategy for all the questions you feel vulnerable on.

Here are some approaches to several of the particularly sensitive ones: "What was your last salary?"

This is a loaded question, particularly in the early part of an interview. If you give an answer that is out of the range of the job before you've had a chance to sell yourself, you may have closed the door to the opportunity—or priced yourself under what you should be getting. Try to defer an answer to this question until later on in the interview. You might say something like this, "My salary requirements are somewhat flexible depending on the job and the long-range opportunity. I wondered if we could defer this question until I get a better understanding of the job responsibilities and you know more about my background." When you are forced into discussing the salary question, ask for a salary in line with your last one including your fringe benefits and a reasonable increase.

Your first-tier answer might be "I feel that with my experience I'm worth $60,000" (your last salary plus a reasonable increase). Try to avoid giving your actual salary, although you may be forced to. Make sure you point out any unusual fringe benefits you've been receiving, such as a company car or a club membership. Bear in mind that sometimes a difficult question is asked not to see what your specific answer is, but rather for the interviewer to get a feel for how you handle a tough problem. Prepare an answer to the 15 most important questions you're likely to be asked. Here is a list of particularly sensitive questions:

How well would you work for a younger man or woman?

How long have you been out of work?

What have been your biggest failures?

What would you change about yourself?

Aren't you overqualified?

Where do you want to be five years from now? Where do you think you'll be?

What's wrong with your present job?

Does your present employer know you're looking for another job?

Will you be out to take my job?

What have you disliked most about past jobs?

If you were starting out now, what would you
do differently?

Are you willing to relocate?

How important is salary compared to other
aspects of the job?

What three things have you done in your life
that you're most proud of?

Give me some examples of the biggest problems
(or frustrations) of your last job. How did you
resolve them?

Tell me about the best boss you ever had. The
worst.

What kind of criticism has been given you? Was
it deserved? What did you do about it?

Did you ever fail at any job you tried? Why?

What adverse factors have kept you from pro-
gressing faster?

What does the word *success* mean to you?

You should be prepared for some very personal
questions, even though they're unlikely to be
asked. For example:

What do you and your spouse disagree about?

How large a mortgage do you have? How much
outside income do you have? What are your
savings? Your net worth?

The general areas you're likely to be asked are
about your education, employment history, how
you use your leisure time, your health, community
activities, personal philosophy, finances, your present family life, and even your early family life.

**The company's background**

Get pertinent information on a company, its industry and the person who will be interviewing you before the interview. If a company is publicly held, get its annual report or even an in-depth security analysis from a bank or a broker. The public relations department of many companies is a good source of information. It will often provide you with a company history, recent speeches of top officials, product information, newspaper articles, and so on. Other possibilities are local newspaper or library files, the chamber of commerce, your banker, your accountant, or trade magazines. A library with a good business section can also be helpful. For data on an industry, try annual reports of competitors, studies by securities analysts, or trade magazines. This can give you real insight into what's going on in the industry and the problems this company is likely to be facing. Get the background information fast—you often have only a couple of days to prepare for the interview.

Acquiring information on the interviewer is much harder, but in some cases it can be done and can be extremely valuable. Here are some possible sources: personal contact either through a director, a banker, or a friend who may or may not be an employee, or his or her college alumni directory or class report. Many colleges publish biographies of the members of a class at the time of a reunion. They are available through the college alumni office. Standard and Poor's *Register,* Dun's *Reference of Corporate Management,* and *Who's Who* are other sources that may be useful. Your goal in this research is to anticipate the key problems the interviewer has on his or her mind in your field of expertise.

Locating the material on the company and the interviewer is an important part of the task. An hour or two studying it should put you in a strong position. Such things as recent earnings, sales, new products, markets, plants, what competitors are doing, recent performance of the stock, and so on, are particularly pertinent, depending on the job you're seeking. Prepare a list of five or six questions about the company and its problems in your field of expertise. This will get the interviewer talking about his or her problems in connection with the job you're interviewing for and will help you show how valuable your experience is.

**Hidden criteria**

You not only must prepare for the questions you may be asked, but you also must prepare to address hidden criteria likely to be on the interviewer's mind, but which probably won't be brought out in the open. In fact, if there are things you are vulnerable on, you'll want to insert the answers into the conversation, even though the questions aren't asked.

Sam Price, head of the marketing group of a large company, recently showed me the importance of hidden criteria very dramatically. There never has been a woman in this department of over 20 professionals. Sam told me that two or three MBAs are hired every year, and there is an increasing number of women applicants. It is Sam's feeling that a successful employee in this department must show that he or she can compete on a "fast track," enduring a lot of overtime and traveling. It has been the feeling of the department management that such jobs are best filled by men. Sam readily acknowledges that his department's practice is discriminatory (and therefore illegal). But this situation points out that good candidates are blocked by factors the interview doesn't reveal. Furthermore, a candidate, to be successful, must address this undiscussed issue and be able to make a strong case that the liability is more imagined than real.

Hidden criteria can take many forms (for example, concerning the candidate's age, whether he or she will fit, etc.).

Here are some of the unasked questions.

How will this candidate fit in?

What makes this person tick?

Is this applicant really results-oriented?

How long will he or she need to be really effective?

Will lack of experience in this particular field (or industry, or type of organization) be really detrimental?

Will he or she consider this an interim position?

Can this candidate really get things done through others?

What about weaknesses?

What about working well under pressure?

Does this person get angry or easily depressed?

What is the real reason for the present job search?

Will family life or outside activities adversely affect performance?

Why is she or he interested in working for us?

What about communicating with all levels, verbally and in writing?

If such items are things you are vulnerable on, you'll want to introduce the subject yourself in an offhand way. Comparing your job description (Chapter Four) with what you have to offer (Chapter Five) will identify the most likely hidden criteria. For instance, an older executive may defuse the age issue in the following ways:

"I had a good relationship with my boss at Harris Spring. He was 11 years younger than me. He had a lot of new ideas and was willing to take considerable risks. I think he valued my judgment as he often used me as a sounding board. He then modified his plans to prevent them from going awry."

"I play for my club in a tennis league and still ski downhill a lot."

"The last couple of years have been the most exciting of my career. I have accomplished more, worked under greater pressure, and done more traveling than at any time during my career."

**Your references**     A good reference can be a great asset; a poor one can hurt you badly. But even a poor reference can usually be defused by using the proper strategy. Be sure you handle your references with care, and remember that they are most effective when an employer is near to making you an offer.

First of all, get your references' permission to use them. Bring to each interview a list of your references including his or her name, title, address, and phone number. If you have any doubts about a particular reference, you may want to have this individual checked by a third party (acting as someone interested in hiring you). Be careful that such a move is not uncovered—it can backfire. This third-party reference check can be valuable, particularly if your prior company is in turmoil. You may find that a person you are using as a reference is no longer there or his or her function has changed and the inquiry is passed on to somebody who doesn't know that much about you.

If you are certain a key reference is going to be unfavorable and yet it is necessary to use it, prepare employers by revealing ahead of time that they probably will get an unfavorable report and explain why. This is far better than having the employer surprised. Try to get the employer to talk to others at your former company who may be more favorable to your cause. For example, if you were the controller and didn't get along with the vice president of finance, perhaps you had a good relationship with the manufacturing or marketing vice presidents, who can make the vice president of finance's reference less damaging.

If an unfavorable reference was from some time ago, you may want to talk to that person. Time has a way of healing wounds. In retrospect, a former boss may have realized later the difficulty of your former position. Seeing such a reference personally will probably be more effective than a phone call. Use your references sparingly, only when an employer is near to making you an offer. Finally, you may want to inform a reference about a particular job you are being considered for so that he or she can make the most favorable presentation for you. You may also want to coach the reference by explaining the biases and interests of the person who will be calling.

**Your interview plan**

One common complaint of many job hunters in coming out of an interview is, "I really busted that interview. If I had a chance to do it over again, I would have. . . ." The best way to overcome this failing is to develop a plan for each interview in advance. Make up a checklist of the key items you want to get across on one or two 3 x 5 cards: your major accomplishments and skills, five or six questions you want to ask the employer to focus the interview on problems associated with the job you're seeking, and finally the questions you're most vulnerable on so that you are well prepared to overcome them.

Review these cards just before the interview so that you have your strategy well in hand. Also have these cards handy during the interview for quick reference. A final step of interview preparation is to review a checklist prepared from the answers to the question, "Knowing what you do now, what would you have done differently?" from your "Post-interview Analysis" of each interview to date (see Figure 10-1). Try to get a few mock interviews with a friend or two before you start the whole interviewing process. Ask your friends to make them as realistic as possible. In developing your answers to questions and your presentation of your PARs you may find it useful to talk into a tape recorder to listen to how you sound.

Now let's see how you should conduct yourself in the interview.

# Chapter ten

# THE ART OF INTERVIEWING— IMPROVING YOUR EFFECTIVENESS

**Interview theory**

Remember Betty Black? She was frustrated when, after reviewing the resumes of more than 100 applicants for a computer manager's job, she couldn't find a single candidate worth interviewing. Later on the personnel department referred six candidates to her.

Several interviews provided Black with insight into the key elements of the interview process. Two of the candidates quickly eliminated themselves from contention. Black often started an interview with the typical icebreaker, "Why don't you tell me something about yourself." One candidate took more than 10 minutes to answer. He emphasized a lot of irrelevant personal history and hardly touched on how his experience might be helpful to Black. The second candidate related at length how she had been responsible for the successful installation of a new procedure on her former company's computer. Unfortunately for this candidate, the procedure was of minor importance to the kind of business that Black was in. In addition, this candidate's presentation of her background emphasized that she came from a highly specialized industry quite unlike Black's. Here again, Black right away saw the candidate as a poor fit.

On the other hand, Ray Jarvis, the successful candidate (and from the same industry as the second unsuccessful candidate), took a completely different approach. Jarvis divulged as little about himself as possible at first. By asking questions about likely problems, he got Black to reveal some things about what she was looking for in a candidate. Then Jarvis presented the parts of his background that seemed to meet Black's needs as much as possible. Jarvis found out that Black's company had a relatively new computer installation. Jarvis asked the obvious question, "Well, how is it going?" By this time Black was so frustrated over her computer problems and her inability to find good candidates for her manager's job that she blurted out, "It's a mess! Our costs are much higher than expected, there are lots of delays in getting reports out, and we have far too many errors." What an opportunity this presented for Jarvis! Jarvis grabbed it—he explained how he had successfully dealt with each of these three problems in the past. Black recognized that she was interviewing a strong candidate for the job. After two more interviews she hired him.

This incident reveals clearly the key aspects of interviewing from your point of view. First, get the employer to reveal what he or she is really looking for. Second, present your past experience in a convincing way to show that you can meet the employer's needs.

Jarvis conveyed three things to Black:

1.  He had a pretty good understanding of Black's problems.
2.  He had experience in solving similar problems.

3. By his manner he demonstrated that he had a desire to help Black solve these problems.

The objective of both interviewer and applicant is to achieve a mutual understanding of how well the job requirements and the applicant's qualifications fit. When this is achieved, then the interview will be most effective. While it may not seem so on the surface, this statement is equally true even though the applicant may not get the job, because it is of little real benefit to the applicant in the long run if he or she is hired for a job that is unsuitable.

To take this concept one step further, let's look at the mutual objectives in an interview from the applicant's and then the employer's standpoint:

1. The applicant's objectives: (*a*) to find out if this is a desirable job; and (*b*) if so, to convince the interviewer that he or she is the best candidate.
2. The employer's objectives: (*a*) to find out if the applicant is the best person for the job; and (*b*) if so, to persuade the applicant to take the job.

As an applicant, your first objective is not necessarily to get the job. First find out enough about it to determine if it is right for you. If it is, *then* your objective is to get the job. There is one exception to this. If you've been out of a job for a long time, try to get an offer anyway. Maybe you won't accept it, but at least it's a great boost to your morale.

**The actual interview**

Get to each interview at least 10 minutes before your appointment. This gives you an opportunity to observe the surroundings, as well as to review your notes and have some time to relax. Reread your resume—it is the prime piece of background information that the employer already has about you—and it is so easy to forget some of the things in it. Also review the 3 x 5 cards which are your interview plan, including the five or six key questions you have developed to find out what the employer really wants. Once in a while you will run into an aggravating problem—you are on time for the interview but the employer doesn't call you in for a half hour or more. Keep your cool—the delay may be caused by a genuine crisis. But if it results from poor planning on the part of the employer, keep this in mind before you accept any job offer.

Make sure that your appearance is in keeping with what an employer is looking for. A good rule of thumb is to emulate the appearance of the top professionals in your field.

Most applicants assume that an interview starts when they meet the interviewer. In most cases that is true. However, the interview can be considered to start with the interviewer's secretary, or even the receptionist.

Don't worry about being nervous—it's natural and it will keep you alert. When you are introduced to interviewers, look them straight in the eye, shake hands firmly, and smile. Their office is their home— so let them call the tune. Wait until they invite you to sit down and indicate where you are to sit. Expect some small talk about the weather, sports, or current events. Observe the things that interviewers have in their office—pictures and mementos. These can be clues to their interests and can provide the means for building some rapport in this preliminary stage.

Some students of the interview process believe that the first 10 minutes are critical—that is, many candidates are rejected in that time, with the balance of the interview providing the interviewer with the justification for this decision. In a boxing match, contestants ordinarily spend the early part of the fight feeling each other out, probing for strengths and weaknesses. A similar approach in a job interview puts you in the position of controlling it. It is important to quickly determine what key things the employer is looking for. It is helpful to visualize the main part of the interview as a three-stage process:

*1. Identifying the employer's needs.* Your objective in this stage is to get employers to reveal as much as possible about what they are looking for in the person they will hire—the problems to be solved, what has already been done to solve them without success, their priorities, the kind of experience they're looking for, their personal biases, and so on. Employers will usually start by asking for some general information such as, "Tell me about yourself," or "Tell me about your last job." You have already seen how the first two applicants for the computer-manager job made the mistake of misinterpreting this. Betty Black's primary purpose was to get background information about the applicant. The applicant then had an opportunity to establish an immediate positive image. You can do this by skimming over your background and providing the interviewer with what he or she would like to hear. End with a statement of benefits the employer can expect if you are hired. For example:

"I have been fortunate to have a good education—a B.S. in mechanical engineering from Purdue. I have had 19 years of production experience, most recently as general manager of the Elkhart Division of Consolidated Machinery—a division with 1,200 employees. I feel I've been successful in solving a wide variety of problems working as a team member with other key people. I have worked hard and have been stimulated by challenge. My goal has always been to deliver what I promise on time and within budget. What are the problems here?" An alternative ending might be "My objective is to help you find out what you want to know about me. How do you want to begin?"

*2. Selling yourself.* Once the employer identifies a problem, relate a PAR to show your experience and skills in coping with a similar problem. For example, if the employer reveals that a key problem is cutting costs, relate one or two experiences showing that you have done this consistently, with considerable resourcefulness and leadership.

Here is where your preparation will pay off. Drawing on your research on the company, what you may have heard about the job and the interviewer, and your own hunches, ask the most appropriate of the five or six questions that you have prepared. Depending on the reply, follow up with several other questions. The answers will give you the framework of what the employer is looking for in a candidate. If you don't do this, you may spend a lot of time on subjects that aren't of real interest to the employer. If you are not sure of the kind of thing that the interviewer is looking for, you might ask, "Would you like to hear about my experience in X or in Y?" Such a question requires the interviewer to give you direction. Note that phases one and two are not distinct in themselves but are overlapping. In fact, these two stages essentially consist of a series of stages one and two, with the employer revealing a need and the applicant showing his or her experience in satisfying the need and then directing a query to get the employer to reveal another need.

If you are asked how you would solve a particular problem, be careful. You're treading on thin ice if you give the impression you know the solution. After all, the employer probably has had somebody working on it before without reaching a satisfactory solution. Very likely any solution you suggest has been tried without success. You'll create a much more favorable impression if you state that you'd have to study the situation to learn what has already been done, why a satisfactory resolution hasn't been achieved, and what subtleties have prevented more progress. Then go on to describe how you successfully coped with a similar problem elsewhere, emphasizing the careful planning and the development of the needed cooperation and follow-through that resulted in the solution.

Another key to building rapport with the employer is to show sensitivity to his or her hang-ups. As you've already seen, employers often put as much stress on personal attributes as on technical qualifications. Try to find out what the employer feels is important—getting work done on time, keeping him or her informed, being a stickler for details are typical items. Show by your PARs that you can deal with these things.

Also, provide answers to the questions the interviewer should ask, but may not (and which you may need to answer).

*3. Conclusion.* As the interview is drawing to a close, be sure to ask these two key questions. "Where do we have a fit? Where don't we have a fit?" This invariably brings to light one or two reservations the interviewer has about you.

Charles Burke was a 53-year-old superintendent of Miracle Adhesives. In interviewing Frank Stewart, he was favorably impressed but wondered whether or not Stewart had the experience to deal effectively with the union. When Stewart questioned Burke, this lack of experience with unions was pointed out. It was easy for Stewart to show that his two years as a first-line supervisor of an assembly operation involved extensive dealings with the United Auto Workers and that he had upheld the company's interests effectively. Stewart believes that presenting this experience was a key reason why he was offered the job.

As the interview draws to a close, if there is a

mutuality of interest, get a clear understanding of
what the next steps are. Try to get as definite an
answer as possible from the interviewer. The key
thing you want to learn is when he or she might
next be in touch with you, and when it would be
appropriate for you to make a follow-up call.
Watch for signs that the employer wants to end the
interview. Don't overstay your welcome.

Your strategy in subsequent interviews should be
similar to the first. Your goal in each is to get the
next interview until you get an offer. You can tell
the employer's increasing interest as this process
evolves by certain actions on his or her part. Basically there will be a subtle change from an imper-
sonal to a more personal relationship. Some of the
tipoffs to watch for are:

The employer:
— Discusses problems freely, sometimes revealing
  confidential matters.
— Introduces you to other company executives.
— Starts to sell the company to you.
— Extends the interview beyond an understood
  deadline or instructs his or her secretary to
  hold all calls.
— Starts to take an interest in you as a person,
  talking about his or her family and interests,
  or inquiring about yours.

Your behavior should be guided by the employer's, but make sure never to overstep any
bounds. Reading into an employer's actions a more
familiar relationship than is intended could be
damaging.

Actual job interviews in the visible market are
more structured than those in the hidden market,
and you will have less opportunity to influence
their direction. Very likely you will have to do pro-
portionately more of the talking. However, the

same general principles apply, namely, good preparation and trying to find out the interviewer's needs by asking good questions and responding to them using your PARs.

**The interviewer**     Bear in mind a few general thoughts about the role of the interviewer. Understanding them can help you develop your interviewing skill.

Interviewers are in a difficult spot. With limited exposure to applicants, they must make choices that can considerably affect their own job performance and influence the opinions people in the organization have about them. In these circumstances, they ordinarily will choose a safe candidate in contrast to a controversial one, because they have much less at risk personally if the person is not successful. Furthermore they have other pressing priorities on their minds—often problems on which they are being pushed for immediate decisions. The favorable result from hiring the right people, getting them on board and functioning effectively, has its payoff months away, at least. Thus, often their inclination is not to hurry the process.

Generally, though, people think that all of the advantages are in the hands of the employer. This is because the interview is being held on the employer's turf, the employer knows the requirements of the job, and he or she has the job to offer.

Actually, you as the applicant have some key advantages too. First of all, employers are usually busy people. They recognize the need for their considerable involvement in the hiring process although they probably won't consider it a top priority. However, as soon as they can make a decision on who they want to hire, this problem is solved and they can devote their time to more immediately important things. As every applicant comes through the door, the employer is hoping against hope that this one will be the successful candidate. Besides, if you're conducting an active campaign, you're involved in job interviews every day. After a while you can become pretty skilled in handling them, far more so than many employers will be. Finally, you can spend time to zero in on your target so that you can find out a lot about the company and even the interviewer. Very rarely does an interviewer do this in-depth investigation of an applicant in the early stages. Thus, you have greater opportunity to be well prepared about the situation you're liable to face in an interview, and can deal with it most effectively.

There are a number of different types of interviewers that you may encounter, so be ready for all of them. Regardless of the type, if you don't cope with the interviewer effectively, you are the loser. The more important and frequently met types are:

The friendly type—you may have what seems to be a very good interview with this kind of individual, but it may be ineffective for you, because you haven't had a real opportunity to get across what's most important to your cause. Be prepared to speed up the pace of the interview, to shortcut your plan (if necessary), so you can discuss the job requirements and your qualifications adequately.

The third-degree type—this is the kind of individual who tries to create a stress situation in an interview to see how effectively you can deal with it. He or she may use a series of rapid-fire questions that are somewhat unrelated, or play games—like remaining silent for some time—just to see how you will handle the situation. Your best approach is to keep cool and to relieve the stress by asking questions. There are few individuals who in a one-on-one situation will not respond to a question.

The disorganized type—here is someone who may create some of the same problems as the friendly type. For example, you may find yourself coming out of the interview without having had a real opportunity to get yourself across. It is quite likely that this interviewer has not clearly thought out what he or she is looking for. Raising your five or six questions and the X or Y alternative question, should get this type of interviewer to better define what he or she is looking for. Again be ready to speed up your plan.

The reserved type—such an individual's style makes it difficult to avoid doing most of the talking and to find out what type of person he or she is looking for. You must be persistent in probing for this. Using the questioning technique almost always will reveal his or her needs in time.

The ego-tripping type—here is an individual who is so strongly self-centered that he or she will take a good part of the interview trying to impress *you*. With these individuals, you may be the loser unless you take the initiative to get them to define what they're looking for. Here again you may have to speed up your plan.

**Other people in the company**  If you are scheduled for an interview with one or more individuals at a level comparable to your prospective boss, you are getting more than casual consideration. Your approach to each of them should be similar to the way you approached your prospective boss, except that such interviews ordinarily are not as in depth. A middle-of-the-road approach is to ask the interviewer which of the different parts of your experience he or she would like to learn more about. Obviously you should use the opportunity in each of these conversations to give the person the most favorable picture of your background as it relates to the job requirements. This is true of a personnel executive as well as other key line or staff executives. Such interviews offer a particularly good opportunity to explore each interviewer's view of the job. You may get a somewhat different picture from them about the job requirements or why the job is open. It may be that these other executives have a more objective picture of the job than the boss, who may be anxious to hire you and doesn't want to dampen your interest. Be wary of taking the job if there is a strong divergence of views about it among the various people you talk to, unless these differences are resolved.

If you can establish rapport with your prospective boss's secretary, he or she can be helpful, particularly in the follow-up phase. Try to find some common interests to make a favorable impression. Some people have found a thank-you note will do this. A favorably-inclined secretary can handle your follow-up calls, inform you generally how things are going, and see to it that your interest is brought to the boss's attention at a favorable time.

Ask the secretary for the full names, nicknames, special pronunciations, and titles of all the key people you see.

**Courtesy interviews**

A courtesy interview is one where there is little likelihood of an open job. But it is an opportunity to meet an important person who can provide you with information and referrals to other key individuals or companies. Usually you will not be sure in advance whether or not your meeting will be a job or courtesy interview. Until you know otherwise, you should assume it is an actual job interview. So your primary goal is to develop the employer's interest in hiring you. Your objectives in courtesy interviews are as follows:

1. A lead to an actual job.
2. Referrals—the names of (and preferably an introduction to) *people who can hire you.*
3. Information—about the field, companies, people, salary ranges, and so on.
4. Leaving a good impression for a future job.

For a courtesy interview you should undergo the same type of preparation (but not as intense) as for an actual job interview. You should explain to the interviewer why you feel it is important for you to talk and the help that you would like to get from him or her. If the person has made it clear that there isn't a job, make it clear you understand this. It will considerably reduce the tension. A resume can be a useful tool here because it provides a summary of the highlights of your background. It is often useful to ask the interviewer for a reaction to it. Another useful line of questioning, after he has reviewed your resume, is to get a reaction to your objective based on your background. You should then pursue the objectives of a courtesy interview as described above. If it is at all possible, you should try to get at least three referrals, and get the interviewer's agreement that you can use his or her name as an introduction to them. Always send a brief thank-you note, even if it is handwritten.

If the interview has been particularly useful to you, you will want to lay the groundwork for following it up. One useful way of gaining favor is to send a short note describing what resulted from each one of the referrals he or she gave you. Perhaps every month afterward you should phone and ask him if he has any further thoughts.

**Follow-up after the interview**

What do you do after the interview? Most job hunters feel that about all you can do is hope for the best. But there are a number of things you can do to enhance your image. And since these are done so infrequently, you have an unusual opportunity to show that you stand well above the crowd.

If your interview was for a job you really want, regardless of how unsatisfactory the interview was, don't give up on it. Many a job has been landed by resourceful follow-up, in spite of an apparently unfavorable first interview. Appropriate action at this stage will very likely improve an employer's regard for you, because it shows a number of the characteristics that he or she is looking for: determination, perseverance, and resourcefulness. As you will recall, follow-up activities include analysis of the interview, a thank-you letter, and keeping third parties such as referrers or recruiters informed. Another step, depending on the interview, is to research possible solutions to problems that the employer outlined in the interview. Follow this by a hard-sell follow-up letter and a telephone call.

Executive jobs often take a long time to fill. Inaction is not necessarily a turndown. Furthermore, a turndown is not necessarily final.

Immediately after each interview, take 10 minutes to fill out a "Post-interview Analysis" report, a copy of which is shown in Figure 10-1. Information there can be useful in making your follow-up letter most effective and in improving your interviewing skill. Within two days make sure that you send a thank-you letter, an example of which is shown in Figure 10-2. Observe particularly that there is a paragraph which brings up some subjects that you had not been able to get into the interview. This thank-you note should be typewritten, except in the case of a friend when a short handwritten note is acceptable. Not only does a thank-you provide a means to present your experience again, but it probably puts you in the small minority. A follow-up letter after each subsequent interview provides an additional opportunity for you to

**FIGURE 10-1**
Post-interview analysis

Be as specific as possible.

Date _____ Length of interview _____

Who _____
Be sure of spelling and title, nickname; list all key people; make note of any important interests, personality traits, biases; name of interviewer's secretary.

Where _____
Company, address, division, etc.

Your objectives _____

Company's objectives _____

Summary of important things interviewer said (advice, criticism, names, problems, plans, job requirements, "hot buttons" or areas of special interest, personal interests, closing remarks, etc.). Be specific.

Summary of things you said that got strongly positive or receptive reaction (opening remarks, points emphasized, sensitive areas, etc.).

What are the principal requirements of this job (i.e., what problems are you expected to solve, what are the yardsticks for measuring performance)?

How was follow-up left?

What do you think his or her reservations are about you?

FIGURE 10-1 *(continued)*

What is your perception of interviewer (Did he or she put you at ease? Is he or she a stickler for detail, etc.?)

What can you do now to make a favorable impression (e.g., research—on questions he or she raised and needs answers to; useful suggestions, etc.)?

Who (if anybody) should you inform about the interview?

Include in hard-sell follow-up letter:

Corrections:

Additions:

Research:

Reminders:

Ask for:

Did you get referrals (if interview didn't work out)?

If interview was a result of referral from a third party, should you get feedback from the third party?

How would you rate your interview performance?

Excellent _____          Poor _____

Good _____          Very poor _____

Satisfactory _____

**FIGURE 10-1** *(concluded)*

If you had a chance to have the interview over again, knowing what you do now, what would you do differently?

In preparation?

In interview?

---

**FIGURE 10-2**
Thank-you letter immediately after a first interview

April 28, 1981

Mr. Frank A. Joyce
Chief Financial Officer
American Foods Company
735 Seventh Avenue
New York, NY 10918

Dear Mr. Joyce:

Thank you
    It was a pleasure to talk with you Monday afternoon. I appreciate your candor and believe I came away with a good understanding of your position of Controller. It appears to be a wonderful opportunity to apply the financial control experience I had over the years at Superior Biscuit.

Review of highlights
    In our discussion, you clarified the goals and the duties of the position. I am well aware of the importance you place in standardizing the controls and financial reporting system of the seven plants of Peerless you recently acquired in the merger with your current system. Also I understand the need you feel for changing your cost accounting to a standard process cost system.

Your capabilities related to his needs
    I have given considerable thought to the needs and challenges you have and feel that my overseeing this type of changeover at Mid Atlantic for a year and a half indicates I can win cooperation and achieve results quickly. That we

FIGURE 10-2 *(continued)*

made three acquisitions at Superior in seven years shows I have dealt with the problems of acquisitions. The third was far and away the most complex and yet we were able to effect it in less time than all the others.

**New information**     At the end of our talk you alluded to your concerns of American's needs to control construction and research costs. I didn't get a chance to outline the construction management system I installed at Superior, covering not only control of progress of the work but its costs. Overseeing our last three construction projects was my "baby," and we were able to complete two of them ahead of schedule and under budget. The other one ran 3 percent over estimate and was behind schedule two months, mainly due to the extreme cold in the winter of 1977-78. I also revised our control of research projects with similar success.

**Ask for action**     In conclusion, I feel I am well qualified for the position and am very interested in it. It is just the kind of long-range opportunity I am seeking. I look forward to hearing from you next week about another chance to get together. If I don't hear from you by the 15th, I will call to see where matters stand.

I appreciate your time and interest.

Sincerely,

sell yourself and to show that you are a careful, caring professional.

Executive recruiters expect you to inform them promptly of the progress of each interview. Again, doing so is not only for their benefit; it often can help your cause and show you how your candidacy is going. Informing referrals of progress can also help your cause.

Few job hunters use what they learn in an initial interview to do things that can make a favorable impression in a second interview or after a turndown. For example, if you are interviewed for a job in a retail operation, visit one or more of the company's stores and observe things from the boss's standpoint. Very likely you will see things that could be questioned. In the industrial sales field, you could call on several customers or potential customers, representing yourself as being interested in working in the field or as a consultant working for a competitor of the company that interviewed you. From this you might get some very useful information that could be used to indicate to an employer that you have the company's interests in mind and that you have insight into its problems.

Harry Gray, whose prior job as president of a miniconglomerate paid well over $100,000 a year, spent more than 40 hours between interviews with Belair Plastics dissecting its annual report and its 10-K, and talking with bankers, investment analysts, and so on. His homework paid off—he was shortly offered a vice presidency at Belair.

Cliff Butler learned in his first interview that Realistic Textiles was having trouble arranging new financing. After the interview Cliff made an inquiry with his connections in financial circles about the type of financing Realistic needed. From his research, he developed several possible approaches to this financing problem and impressed Realistic very favorably in a second interview. Such actions put you way ahead of most other candidates.

Usually a round of first interviews with six candidates takes two to three weeks at a minimum. This time span can work to your advantage, especially if you had a poor first interview. During the interim the employer's negative image of you may have faded somewhat as he or she has seen other candidates. Now prepare a careful "upon further reflection" letter, showing your experience in the most favorable light based on what you learned in the first interview. Mailed several weeks after that interview, this sometimes can put you back in the running. In this letter, stress things to which the interviewer responded favorably, positive achievements in areas you were most vulnerable on, things you didn't bring up, and research you've since done on problems the employer outlined in the interview. Figure 10-3 shows an example of such a letter.

**FIGURE 10-3**
**"Upon further reflection" letter two to three weeks after a first job interview**

                                                                Date

Mr. George Smith
Vice President of Sales
Federal Transformer Company
637 Grand Avenue
Cleveland, OH 20704

Dear Mr. Smith:

Recall of
interview

The more I think of the position of Sales Manager of Federal, the more I am excited by it. Not only do I think it is a wonderful opportunity, but I feel that it represents the kind of long-run challenge I am looking for. Your company's goals and the organizational chemistry that I perceived particularly impressed me.

His needs/your
capabilities

My 17 years in sales and sales management, mostly in the electrical industry, has provided me with considerable problem-solving experience that should be very useful to the Federal sales effort at this time. Understandably you expressed great concern for the need for an extensive and quick overhaul of your sales effort. I took over Acme Control's Sales Manager's position four years ago in a downturn similar to what Federal is now experiencing. My first year and a half there I was able to strengthen the sales team so that Acme experienced only a 9 percent decrease in sales as compared to over 21 percent each for its three major competitors. I revised the sales incentive plan and greatly increased the training and upgrading of our requirements for new salesmen. These elements were major factors in this success.

FIGURE 10-3 *(continued)*

That I was able to make this impact at Acme indicates I was able to size up what was needed, and could develop and execute a plan quickly. Yet this wasn't at the expense of future progress, since considerable improvement was made over the next several years. My emphasis on a team approach reduced salesstaff turnover by 55 percent in the first two years.

Your feeling that for the foreseeable future you should have a Sales Manager with long experience in the field makes sense to me. My prior five-year roles were with Peters Cable where I was intimately involved with sales management problems in the field. The last two years as Assistant Sales Manager involved seven trips in which I covered our 17 branch offices and most of our approximately 50 distributorships. The prior three years was as the Chicago Zone Manager, which involved the overseeing of seven district offices and 11 distributorships. Our zone during this period showed a 23 percent gain in sales at a time when the industry was showing only a 6 percent increase. At the time we had a large introduction of new products which required developing greatly increased expertise in our company sales engineering force. It also made greatly increased demands on our field service organization. Our zone was able to decrease customer complaints by 7 percent, while the four other zones in the company averaged increased complaints of over 27 percent.

The broad experience which I gained in these roles would enable me to help Federal solve its current problems of declining sales and increased customer complaints in line with your goals.

New information

I don't recall mentioning a follow-up and control system which I developed to considerably increase the number of new accounts of the company. Nor did I speak of the new uses we engineered for our transformers at Acme in the paper industry, which enabled us to make substantial inroads in controls on compressors in this industry for the first time.

Left in question

You will recall we discussed the possibility of distributing your equipment on a lease basis. I have since learned

**FIGURE 10-3** *(concluded)*

that two of the large machine tool manufacturers (Perfection and Baltimore Grinding) recently started to do this. Perhaps it would make sense for you to contact them on their program.

Research
While your reputation for the highest quality products in your industry seems to continue, do you feel your prominence in service may have slipped? As a pseudo-consultant, I called on half-a-dozen major electrical equipment buyers and found very favorable comments about Marshalls' [a competitor] new warehouse and computerized parts control setup, as contrasted with long delays in parts availability that you and Dominion seem to be plagued with.

Ask for action
I am very interested in the possibility of joining Federal as Sales Manager. I feel that I am well qualified for the position. It sounds like a very challenging role and I would hope that we can meet again and explore the matter in greater depth. I will call you on Friday the 15th, if I haven't heard from you about our next meeting.

Sincerely,

Another aspect of your follow-up is keeping in touch with the employer with periodic phone calls. I know of several applicants who landed excellent jobs after a four-month gap between their first and second interviews. In each case the applicants made follow-up calls every two or three weeks. Continue these calls every several weeks until you are told emphatically you are no longer a candidate or that the job has been filled.

If the
interview fails
If the interview is an obvious mismatch, or the company actually doesn't have a suitable job for you, try to get as much useful information for your campaign and as many referrals as you can. The vast majority of interviews will not result in actual job interest, but they can be extremely useful in

your campaign. Most interviews actually are successful–if used correctly, that is. They can provide you with a *lead* to another interview, useful *information,* or a *learning experience.*

If you feel that you did badly in an interview, don't agonize over it. It happens to the most effective job hunters. If you have an active campaign going, such disappointments can be accepted as part of the process without too much upset because you probably will have several other interviews in prospect. At the very least, an unsuccessful interview can provide a learning experience if you identify the things that went wrong and take steps to correct them for future interviews.

If you have had a lot of interviews which have failed (and few, if any, were successful), ask a couple of people who referred you to interviews to discuss your performance with these employers. Explain that you have had a series of unsuccessful interviews and that it would be extremely helpful if they would discuss the matter candidly with the interviewer and let you know why you did not come across as an effective candidate. You may find that your interview style is turning off employers and discover why this is so. Also review Chapters Five, What Do You Have to Offer?, and Nine, Preparing for Interviews, as well as this one, The Art of Interviewing. You may want to develop your own checklist for interview performance based on your own experience.

**Tests**          Tests used to be a key part of the hiring process of many companies. It still is with some, but it is much less prevalent than before. You may be asked to take tests, but the results are probably not a critical factor in the hiring decision. Point out that you may be rusty on taking such tests–so that your performance may be less favorable than it has been on the job. This to some extent may defuse poor test scores, if they occur. Here are some ground rules to help you.

Don't panic, even though you're rusty, you'll probably do perfectly well.

Make sure that you understand the instructions and the rules. Ask questions about what you are to do on the test, any time limit, and the marking formula. For example, do they deduct incorrect answers from right answers or do they merely count correct answers?

Gear your answer to what you think is wanted.

Make sure you plan your time properly in the tests—people sometimes do badly on them because they spend too much time on some parts and too little on others.

If you fare well in the other aspects of the screening process and do adequately on the tests, the test results will probably have little influence on the hiring decision. But don't treat the test too lightly—if you blow it, you may be reeled off the track.

**Interviewing tips**

1. The prime objective in your first or second interview with a company is to get the next interview. Thereafter your objective is to get an offer. This is particularly true if you are in the early stages of a campaign or have been on a campaign for some time and have not had an offer. Any offer should do wonders for your morale (even if you don't accept it). But an offer or two that you would seriously consider can be not only a boost to your spirits but can provide a very effective way of springing loose other offers that might be satisfactory. On the other hand, don't try to get offers indiscriminantly just to record notches on your belt.

2. Your strategy is to get the interviewer to do

most (perhaps two thirds) of the talking. Be an intelligent listener and a brief talker. If you tend to be garrulous, work on that. A senior vice president of one of the largest executive recruiting firms in the country sits in on most first interviews between a client and a prospect. He has noticed that, in general, employers are turned off by applicants who do most of the talking in an interview. And he has seen a lot of employers who were favorably impressed by candidates who let the employers do most of the talking. A typical favorable reaction is, "I like him, although I must admit, I have an awful lot of unanswered questions about him."

3. One of your more effective tools is asking intelligent questions. Not only can it prompt the interviewer to give you direction as to what he or she is interested in, but it also can relieve tension if an interviewer is probing in a sensitive area or an area you would rather defer until later.

4. There are two approaches which will be useful in getting across your strong interest in the job: (*a*) several times ask the employer to repeat what he or she has said (it conveys the message that what is being said is really important to you), and (*b*) say once or twice, "Let me see if I understand what you said correctly." (Then go on to repeat as best you can what he or she has just said.) Once again, this is an indirect compliment because you are really saying, "What you've said is very important to me. I want to make sure I understand it."

5. Learn the kind of place this company would be to work in. Talking to your prospective boss and other key officials of the company (usually on company premises) offers a good opportunity to judge this. Be particularly observant of how people relate to each other. Unquestionably this is a time when these individuals are on their best behavior. Does the atmosphere seem to be tense—or sloppy—or friendly and businesslike? If the

interviewer—say it's George Smith—would be your boss, evaluate him. Is he the kind of person you could be happy working for? Identify the three to five key traits that you see in him. You will want to compare these traits later with people with similar traits you have worked closely with. Don't expect adverse traits to improve. They'll undoubtedly get worse. Make sure your evaluation of the interview is based on your observations, not just what he says. George Smith may describe himself as a "big-picture man," but your observations show him really to be a stickler for details.

6. Keep to your interview plan as much as possible.

7. Don't hesitate to take notes on your interview plan into the interview. Referring to these notes occasionally will indicate that you've given careful consideration to what you want to get out of the interview and what you want to get across. As long as you don't use them as a crutch, they will convey that you are a careful and thorough person. And don't be afraid to record notes on key aspects of the discussion as it proceeds.

8. A job interview is like an athletic contest in which you are a winner or a loser—either you've made a favorable enough impression to get an offer or the next interview, or you haven't. Some job hunters give up the struggle too early. Good athletes and athletic teams consistently find a way to turn a likely defeat into a victory. Good salespeople are successful because they know how to make that second effort. Part of their success stems from their positive frame of mind, a determination not to be defeated, and their skills at turning a faltering interview around. Work on developing this. When an interview has been unsuccessful, try to figure out a way or ways to change the course of such a situation in the future.

9. Probe gently into basic company problems

(such as, the industry is currently in a slump; the company, or the specific job, has high turnover; or the company is having major problems with introducing a new product). This gets across to the interviewer that you have some concerns about the company. You have laid the groundwork to be in a stronger negotiating position for improving an offer if it is made to you. This line of questioning will also clarify the situation in the company to help you decide whether or not you'll want to work there if you get an offer.

10. Make sure interviewers understand your points. If you do not get a favorable reaction when you describe some of your strongest experiences, perhaps you're assuming that they understand the full impact of them, when they really don't. Try extending your description of one or two of your PARs to make them more dramatic, even if you feel it's somewhat overdone. It may bring a more favorable reaction. Here again your PARs will be a big help.

11. Some feel that it is better not to take your resume into an interview, because most conventional resumes raise more questions than they answer. Sometimes you're better off to write a tailor-made resume after the interview. If you didn't use your resume to get the interview, this is probably good advice. Also, this avoids the situation where the interviewer concentrates so much on your resume as to impede the free flow of conversation.

12. Don't criticize your old company. That raises questions about your ability to overcome a setback, and the employer is likely to think "What will this applicant be thinking about our company in time if he or she comes to work for it?"

13. Don't bring up controversial subjects. When the interviewer brings them up, steer the conversation back to something else as soon as you can.

Don't be argumentative—neither should you always agree with the interviewer. Either extreme is a sign of weakness. It is a sign of strength, on the other hand, to disagree at times but in a tactful way, by saying something such as, "Yes, I agree with you, but . . ." (then proceed to make your point).

14. Always conduct yourself as if you are really interested. Don't lounge in your chair. Leaning forward projects your interest and forces you to be alert.

15. Look the interviewer straight in the eye fairly frequently, and be human and smile from time to time.

16. Be businesslike—friendly, and reasonably relaxed. Be yourself. Don't try to act differently because it would be hard to carry it off effectively.

17. Experiment with your interviewing techniques. No one approach will be effective in all types of interviews. If you are carrying on an active and successful campaign, you'll have a fair number of interviews. This makes any single one less important—so you can afford to take some risks in experimenting with your approach. You'll learn what is most likely to be effective for you in any type of situation.

18. When interruptions occur in an interview they upset the continuity of the conversation. Pick up what was being discussed and complete the subject; then go on to ask another question.

19. Be on the lookout for small talk. Here again, you have to use your own judgment. There will be appropriate times for it, such as at the beginning or end of an interview, at lunch, or when you are being walked to somebody else's office. Let the interviewer decide how far this small talk will go. However, it can be a trap if it goes on too long in the interview itself. If you feel this is happening, your best tactic is to ask a question about the job.

20. Samples of your work can be a useful selling

tool. For example, a marketing plan or a major recommendation can be used to show the depth of your thinking, your organizing ability, and so on. This is provided it doesn't breach confidentiality.

21. An employer or a recruiter may try to "interview" you on the phone. They will ask a few leading questions to classify you as a prospect. Such questions might be: "What was your last salary?" "How much experience have you had in X activity?" "How long have you been out of work?" Such questions put you on the defensive and don't give you the chance to learn about the job. Try to avoid being interviewed on the phone. But if you must be, emphasize that your salary is negotiable. Then stress that such sensitive items can best be addressed in a personal interview—and take the offensive by suggesting a time for it.

Now, having covered preparation and interviewing, let's talk about building and maintaining momentum.

# Chapter eleven

# BUILDING AND MAINTAINING MOMENTUM

You have developed your campaign plan. You have completed your resume, developed your letters, prepared your top-priority list of contacts, and brushed up on the art of interviewing. Now you must start your campaign intensively and build momentum to sustain it.

You have already seen that job hunting uses some of the skills you've developed on your job, but it also requires new ones. Working hard at your campaign will develop all the skills you need for job hunting, and you will quickly show improvement if you conduct your campaign actively and interpret the results properly.

**What to expect**  From what you've heard of job hunting in the past you may approach it with some trepidation. Most job hunters do. You may be concerned that you will not see any positive results quickly. As a matter of fact, you may find the opposite is the case. In the early stages you probably will be contacting people you know quite well, and you will find them receptive, full of ideas, and willing to refer you to other important people. Through this process you will be developing a lot of potential opportunities, which may surprise you. (The real surprise usually comes later, when you find out that most of these apparent opportunities either disappear quickly or turn out to be completely unsuitable. This doesn't mean that you shouldn't pursue them—you should, but just remember that most of them will not pan out.)

Be prepared for indignities that you have never experienced—frequent rejection, disdain by some people because you are looking for a job, criticism of your record, having to reveal personal information such as your salary, and feeling uncomfortable in social situations because you're out of work. Also you're going to feel uncomfortable among some of your friends; some may seem quite cool toward you. The plain fact is that you may make them feel awkward, because they don't know how to help—as much as they'd like to.

When you're turned down by a prospective employer, you may feel it's because they regard you as incompetent. But in most cases, it's actually because they have no need for someone like you. (Although it may be because you have done an ineffective job of identifying the employer's need and convincing him or her you can fill that need very well.)

These indignities may discourage you. If so, that's unfortunate—they won't go away. What they should do instead is make you *indignant*. This is a positive thing—particularly if the feeling is channeled into redoubling your determination to make your campaign a success. You will have uncovered one of your greatest resources when you have developed this attitude: "I'm tired of being pushed around. I know I'm good. I've got the record to prove it. Some company is going to be damn lucky to hire me." This change in attitude happened to

Bill Jackson (see Chapter Five). It caused him to delve into his subconscious to discover marketable experience he hadn't recognized. It forced him to become more aggressive and resourceful and to take greater risks in his contacts and interviews.

You are under a lot of pressure—so you'll feel unusual emotional ups and downs. A job that looks about to break for you one week will disappear the next. Conversely, something that has been dormant for a month will become active again. A particularly critical time may occur a month or two after you have started making your initial contacts, because the quality and number of referrals will dwindle and you may be left with very few (if any) possibilities after a very active initial flurry.

Your best approach for minimizing the lows and recovering from them fastest is making new initiatives a key part of your daily routine. Having a lot of activity means you're always looking forward to a number of possible jobs so that if one falls through it isn't as crushing a blow as not having anything in prospect.

The specific job goal that you started off with may be replaced by one that is somewhat different. As you expose yourself to a variety of different possible careers and job possibilities, your perspective of yourself will come into sharper focus, as will your view of what jobs are realistically possible for you. This can be a disappointment if your dream job now appears to be unattainable. Actually, this sharpening of your self-understanding is very valuable—through it you will develop a more realistic set of job requirements which, in time, should result in your finding a job that is really more suitable to your long-term needs. As wide as your acquaintanceship and your general knowledge of a variety of jobs are in the beginning, you will find that your understanding of possible jobs has been quite narrow. Expand your view.

If your search drags on for some months, you may worry that the longer you're out of a job the less marketable you become. However, if you are putting on an active and effective campaign, are being considered for several good opportunities, and are developing new leads, this should not greatly concern you. You probably are making good progress—so stick with your search (and don't panic) until you find a job that meets a high percentage of your requirements.

Finally, you may be surprised how long it takes to get an offer on a specific job. Sometimes it can be three or four months from your first interview to an offer. This is particularly true if there is little urgency on the company's part—for example, if you'd be hired to replace someone who is retiring a year or more from now. Delays like this can easily take place if several company executives are involved in making the choice. If that happens, be persistent, but not obnoxious, and make routine follow-up calls every two to three weeks.

**Use of time**

A key asset for you is time—learn to use it effectively. If you are out of work, job hunting should be a full-time job, 40 hours a week. But if you try to spend 60 hours a week at it, you may end up by being much less effective. Don't sit around the house all day. You may make a very unfavorable impression on a possible employer or recruiter if you are found at home in the middle of a working day. Also you cannot make the most effective use of your time at home. Running an intense campaign with a lot of activity keeps you sharp. Minimize the opportunity to feel down in the dumps. Your typical day should consist of: courtesy and job interviews (at least one a day and sometimes two, or even three), prospecting for new interview possibilities, follow-up on contacts you haven't been able to reach or interviews that you have already had, doing research on the companies and backgrounds of employers of upcoming interviews, writing letters of thanks to people you have seen in the last day or two, and keeping your most fruitful contacts informed of developments on leads they have given you.

Don't waste time on jobs that are completely unacceptable. On the other hand, those that are only mediocre should be pursued as time is available. There is always a chance that one of these will be improved enough to make it a good possibility for you.

Be careful not to get sidetracked. It's easy to waste time running down blind alleys. Usually when people take nine months or more to get a job and have been working hard at it, they have wasted three or four months pursuing inappropriate leads. If you find yourself spending a great deal of time on a lead because it seems exciting to you, make sure that you spend every spare moment developing other possibilities.

Large blocks of time can slip away on what turn out to be fruitless activities. A certain amount of this is inevitable. But make sure that you spend as much time as possible working toward your specific goals. The "Failure Analysis Tool," discussed below, will help you do this.

There are seasonal slowdowns in hiring, such as the summer months of July and August. The hiring process does go on, but there are a variety of delays when key people take vacations. Thus, a process that might take two weeks to a month often can extend to two months or more. The longer it goes on the greater the risk for the applicant (for example, developments within the company may reduce the need for the job being filled, other good applicants may come to light, etc.). The last two weeks in August through Labor Day are a particularly heavy time for vacations. Another slow period is from the middle of December until after January 1. These seasonal delays don't mean that you should stop your campaign altogether, but use your judgment.

You should always run scared (but not panicky). Don't assume that any unknown is going to work out favorably. Assume even good prospects are not going to work out, and continue your efforts to get new leads.

**Failure analysis**    For many the most effective tool for controlling time is the *failure analysis* tool. This is a procedure to get you to. challenge your present thinking, to broaden it—and to push you to intensify your efforts. Typically all of us usually take the optimistic view: If we set a reasonable goal and work hard to achieve it, the goal will probably be reached. The failure analysis tool takes the opposite point of view—it assumes you will not be successful in reaching your goal. This tool forces you to visualize where an activity (an interview, a phone call, a follow-up letter, etc.) can go wrong—so you can take steps ahead of time to prevent the failure from happening. With a little practice and by outlining your answers you should be better prepared for the activity. Let's see how it works.

Let's assume you're preparing for a job interview with Jane Teller of Acme. You feel that you are well prepared for it. Now imagine that you have just come out of the interview and you handled it badly. You've just assessed what went wrong and have identified a number of things you wish you had done ahead of time. Fortunately this interview hasn't taken place yet. You do have an opportunity to do additional preparation for the interview. The thinking process can best be understood by reading the following example:

If I fail *in my interview with Jane Teller, of Acme* what will the likely reasons be and what would I wish I had done differently?

| *Likely reasons for failure* | *Wish I had done differently* |
|---|---|
| I didn't know things I should have about Acme and Teller. | Had read Brown Bros. study of recent problems in industry. |
| | Had talked to Jones of Superior (an acquaintance working for a competitor). |
| | Had talked to Graves of Second National Bank. |
| I let Teller concentrate on me rather than on what she needs in job. | Prepared a list of questions to get Teller talking of her problems. |
| | Didn't direct Teller to her greatest interest by asking "Would you rather hear about X or Y?" |
| I didn't find out Teller's reservations about me. | Made sure I asked the questions "Where do we have a fit? Where don't we have a fit?" |
| I didn't learn what steps Teller plans next. | Asked Teller what her timetable is. |

To use the failure analysis tool, write down the question, "If I fail . . . ," and insert the issue being examined (for example, "in my interview with Jane Teller of Acme") and then head the left column, "Likely reasons for failure," and the right, "Wish I had done differently." For this exercise to be effective, it must be done in writing. Before you finish it, ask yourself "Is there any other possible reason for failure?" and "Are there any other things I wish I could have done differently?" If the question is one that comes up frequently (e.g., "Was preparation for interview adequate?") you may want to develop a checklist for the step to be done differently, to which, for each prospective interview, you add additional items unique to the upcoming one or things to watch out for, learned from past interviews.

Failure analysis is also helpful in setting priorities. For example, it can be used to develop a plan to accomplish the most important things for you in a given time period. What things if they aren't done this week would most upset you. Ask yourself, "If I fail this week, what might be the most likely reasons for the failure, and what would I wish I had done differently?"

**Control your campaign**

Careful record keeping can be a great asset for you. Make up a card on the target executive, as suggested in Chapter Eight under "Developing Your List of Contacts." As your campaign proceeds keep a record on each card of each contact, that is, letter, reply, or interview and follow-up. You will also want to note appropriate information on the other people you have had dealings with in each company.

Keep a diary of who you have seen each day and your expenses in a form suitable for tax purposes. Also include the dates of appointments and upcoming follow-ups. A month-at-a-glance calendar is handy for this.

Set up an alphabetical file folder of all employers you have had contact with and include all the notes, letters, and interview records.

By this time you are well aware that a carefully planned and executed campaign is a lot of work. The amount that you can do—and feel you ought to do—will make every week a full one. It's easy to be so busy you lose your perspective. So keep track of your progress, evaluate it, and adjust your plan accordingly. Take an hour or so each week to tally where you stand. A simple way to count the score is to fill out a summary of weekly activity (see Table 11-1). Then take a few minutes to ana-

**TABLE 11-1**
Summary of weekly activity

|  | Date |  |  |  |  |  |  |  |
|---|---|---|---|---|---|---|---|---|
| *Campaign results* |  |  |  |  |  |  |  |  |
| *a.* Hours worked on campaign |  |  |  |  |  |  |  |  |
| Total job interviews |  |  |  |  |  |  |  |  |
| Acceptable firm offers |  |  |  |  |  |  |  |  |
| Firm offers |  |  |  |  |  |  |  |  |
| Hot prospects (prospects you've had at least two interviews with and which offer good chance of an offer) |  |  |  |  |  |  |  |  |
| First job interviews |  |  |  |  |  |  |  |  |
| First job interviews pending |  |  |  |  |  |  |  |  |
| Follow-up letters/phone calls | / | / | / | / | / | / |  |  |
| *b.* Total courtesy interviews (referral, friend, etc.) |  |  |  |  |  |  |  |  |
| Converted to job interviews |  |  |  |  |  |  |  |  |
| Referrals only |  |  |  |  |  |  |  |  |
| Total actual names received |  |  |  |  |  |  |  |  |
| Courtesy interviews pending |  |  |  |  |  |  |  |  |
| Follow-up letters/phone calls | / | / | / | / | / | / |  |  |
| *Contact development by letter/phone, initial approaches since last report* |  |  |  |  |  |  |  |  |
| *a.* Personal contacts |  |  |  |  |  |  |  |  |
| Phone calls/interviews | / | / | / | / | / | / |  |  |
| Letters/interviews | / | / | / | / | / | / |  |  |
| *b.* Cold or new contacts/prospects/targets |  |  |  |  |  |  |  |  |
| Phone calls/interviews | / | / | / | / | / | / |  |  |
| Letters/interviews | / | / | / | / | / | / |  |  |
| *c.* Ads answered/resulting interviews | / | / | / | / | / | / |  |  |
| *d.* Agencies/resulting interviews | / | / | / | / | / | / |  |  |
| *e.* Recruiters/resulting interviews | / | / | / | / | / | / |  |  |

lyze the results and decide how you should modify your efforts.

Using help     Much of your time will be spent contacting people who cannot hire you but who can provide you with leads and information. Handle them delicately. They are usually busy people and other people like yourself are probably contacting them too. Make it easy for them by following these rules:

Don't expect them necessarily to get quick answers for you. If you need more information, try to be as specific as possible (for example, Can you give me an introduction to X? Would you provide me information on Y?). Keep the burden of action in your hands, because too frequently these people are so busy they don't follow through.

Don't be bashful about soliciting help from those who have already been helpful in your campaign. Often a phone call every two to three weeks to one of them is more useful than five personal interviews with others. These people will let you know if you are overdoing it. Periodically review your list of contacts. Have you been overlooking some good ones? The use of *triggers* is a good device for stimulating contacts. "Can you suggest anyone to see at XYZ?" "At Superior Gear?" "In the high technology companies?" "Do you know anyone looking for someone with a strong record in cost reduction?" "Can you suggest a company that is in a turnaround situation?" "A lawyer?" "An accountant?"

Attend any job hunting clinics that you have heard might be useful. Often the clinic itself can be helpful, in addition to the contacts that you make through it. More and more clinics are available, so ask other job hunters or ex-job hunters which are the most helpful. If you find a counselor who impresses you, try to get his or her personal help. Also get together with another job hunter or two periodically and compare notes (exchange ideas or job leads and discuss useful people).

Be visible. Meet all the potentially helpful people you can (at trade association meetings, community and social functions). Though you may be inclined to withdraw from these activities, seek them out aggressively.

**Personal habits**

Reread your resume every day—it's amazing how things come to light that you may have overlooked.

Don't nickel-and-dime on expenses. Obviously this is no time to overdo, but the expenses that most job hunters run up in their campaign are only a small fraction of their lost income. And expenses for such things as typing help, revisions on resumes, travel, and so on, may be the most important expenses you have during your campaign.

If your campaign continues for six months or more, you may want to do a small amount of consulting—so that you can say that you have been working. Keep it small, though—job hunting is your full-time job.

Regular exercise is important; it can work off a lot of emotion. And you can overcome the age barrier by looking fit and vigorous. Also get some diversion through recreation.

**Checklist for a dragging campaign**

If your campaign is not going satisfactorily, review this checklist at the end of each month.

*Attitude.* Are you proud of what you've done? Do you have a clear idea of what you can and want to do? If not, work harder to develop your presentation of your own accomplishments.

Are you bad-mouthing your former employer? This can only hurt you.

*Work habits.* Are you working as hard as possible?

Are you spending (virtually) all of the hours on your job search out of the house?

Are you physically set up to be effective (a good secretary, effective answering of the phone, etc.)?

Are you getting reasonable amounts of recreation and exercise?

Your answer to all of these should be *yes.*

If you had an opportunity to live your last week over again, what would you have done differently in your job-hunting efforts? If you're not using the failure analysis tool, use it.

*Effectiveness of preparation.* Have you carefully defined what your job requirements are and what type of job would be most suitable? If not, review Chapter Three.

Are you sure you know what employers are probably looking for (not only in technical skills but also in personal characteristics and work habits)? If not, review Chapter Four.

Do you feel interviewers are getting a favorable picture of your accomplishments? If not, is it because you haven't identified them adequately, or because you're not presenting them effectively, or both? If you're not effective, review Chapter Five.

Have you had several employers you've approached by blind prospecting contact you spontaneously for an interview? If so, your resume is probably reasonably effective.

If your answer to the above is no, review your resume. Perhaps you should consider getting a good counselor to evaluate it.

When a campaign drags on for a long time, a breakthrough in "getting your act together" often turns a campaign around. It makes it easier for you to get good interviews and increases your effectiveness in them.

Have you been getting a reasonable number of requests for interviews from answering ads? Five percent is a satisfactory rate. If you're not achieving this rate, are you using the advertising-answering technique outlined in the section, "Help Wanted Ads" in Chapter Seven.

Do you know if any of your references are hurting you?

*Number of interviews.* Of the time you've been spending, are at least 75 percent of your efforts directed toward the hidden job market?

Are you getting at least one (and preferably two) referral interviews a day? Are you getting at least one actual job interview a week? You should be. Are you using the referral and/or telephone methods? If you're not getting enough interviews, use one or both of these techniques aggressively.

Are you getting to see more than half the people you approach on the referral method? If not, try people further down in the organization. If this isn't possible, review the section on "Referrals" in Chapter Eight.

Have you experimented with various techniques (broadcast letters, telephone referrals)?

Have you been spending much too much time on one or two job possibilities to the exclusion of prospecting?

Have you analyzed the time spent to get good interviews? Use the method or methods which are most effective in getting the most interviews in the least amount of time.

*Effectiveness of interview.* Are you converting one half of your first interviews for *actual jobs* into second interviews? If not, work on improving your interview techniques.

Are you coming out of interviews feeling you didn't get yourself across effectively? If not, were you well prepared? Did you have a reasonable understanding of the company and its problems before the interview? Did you have five or six questions prepared to get the employer to reveal his or her principal problems in your field of expertise (so you could show how your experience could help)? Or were you unable to control the interview to get your most favorable experience across? Review Chapter Ten.

Did you have a clear understanding of what the interviewer was looking for perhaps a third of the way into the interview?

Are you doing most of the talking? You should be doing less than half of it.

Have you been able to get a good understanding of the interviewer ahead of time?

Are you losing out because of the unasked question (too old, too young, lacking certain experience, etc.)? Are you taking the offensive to combat it?

Are you getting a good reading on the interviewer's biases? Are you responding to them favorably?

Are you asking the third-stage questions ("Where do we have a fit? Where don't we have a fit?").

Have you been writing a carefully prepared sales letter after each interview, based on what you learned about the job?

Have you gotten feedback from any third parties on your interviews? (Your initial contact may be able to provide it.) This can be useful for you, because an employer may be quite candid with the person who referred you, whereas he or she wouldn't be with you.

If you have had quite a few interviews for actual jobs without an offer, try being less aggressive in seeking interviews for a while. Spend more time on interview preparation and interview techniques.

Have you practiced your interview skills—mock

interviews with friends or volunteer counselors? If
you do this, stress to them the importance of their
being (constructively) critical.

Is your physical appearance in line with what
most employers would feel is satisfactory (your
dress, your hair, etc.)?

*Sources of help.* Have you been asking everyone
you have seen (except on actual job interviews) for
information on the most useful people and organizations for job hunters?

Have you contacted most of the people you
know who have conducted a job campaign in the
last few years?

Are you finding secretaries useful sources of information on follow-up?

Are you keeping in regular touch with the people you have found most useful?

When you have built and maintained constructive activity on your campaign, you will probably
get one or more offers. How to decide which one
to take is explained in the next chapter.

# Chapter twelve

# MAKING THE
# DECISION

**Criteria**

Now you're at the point in your campaign which can make it a success or a failure—the time for decision. You have at least one offer that you are seriously thinking about accepting. But we hope you will be successful in getting three good offers. (If you have *only* one good offer, you must make the difficult decision of accepting it or continuing to look while trying to keep the offer open.) Usually getting the first good offer is the toughest. Often one or two jobs you have been negotiating for some time will come to fruition shortly after the first offer. This may "just happen," or it may occur when you tell a promising prospect that you have another offer. Now you must decide on one of them.

The key is deciding which job is *best for you*—which scores best against your main job requirements as you have refined them throughout your campaign. The real measuring stick lies in the future—say five years from now. Will the job you chose seem right then? Don't let your thinking be distorted into accepting what others might think is "the best job," if an alternative would be better *for you.*

Guard against being carried away. Job hunting means selling yourself, but an employer who finds somebody he or she wants to hire will be trying to sell the company just as hard. Often he or she hasn't done as careful an analysis of needs as you have. Furthermore, you have a lot more at risk—your work record and reputation—while an employer is risking only time and money. And if you were frustrated on your old job or you've been out of work for some time, your emotions may cloud your judgment. That is why a systematic and careful analysis of your offer(s) is terribly important.

Here are five steps to take before accepting an offer:

1. Negotiate enough time to be able to arrive at a good decision.
2. Conduct a sweep of all reasonable alternatives to get other offers.
3. Get the information needed to make the decision.
4. If appropriate, negotiate to upgrade the offer(s).
5. Evaluate the final offer(s).

**Stalling offers**    Never accept an offer on the spot; take time to reflect on it. How much time is a reasonable amount to request? For an executive position at mid-career one week should be a minimum; probably you should get two weeks. Often you can obtain even a month or more. The length of time depends on the individuals involved, the urgency, and so on. If the employer won't allow you to think about it for a week at least, this might tell you something about your prospective boss and the company. Do you want to work for someone who appears shortsighted and inconsiderate?

Regardless of how much time you have, you may find it is necessary to ask for an extension of the deadline, but be careful. It's better to ask for ample time in the first place. The time necessary to make a good decision is often considerable—greater than you might think.

How do you stall an offer? You might say something like this: "Thank you very much for the offer. I'm very interested in XYZ. I know it's a very important decision for you, and it's very important for me at this stage in my career. It would be unfortunate for you if I was not the right person for the job. In the same way it is important to me that this be the right job. I think there is a good chance that it is. I would like to think it over. Could I have two weeks? How about my getting back to you on the 15th with an answer?" Don't indicate that you are going to talk it over with your family. Of course you are, but saying so might suggest weakness.

When an offer is made, repeat it item-for-item to make sure that you understand all the terms. If it is not given to you in writing (and it usually isn't), confirm it immediately in writing, stipulating the date you will give an answer.

**Conduct a sweep**

When your first good offer comes, you undoubtedly have a number of job possibilities resting at various stages. Immediately start "a sweep" of the best possibilities to try to bring them to the offer stage as soon as possible. How far you go in using your actual offer to force a decision is a matter of judgment. If you're unlikely to accept the actual offer, don't put too much pressure on the other possibilities. It's a different story though if you have an offer you are going to accept unless a better one comes along. In this case, trying to force a better offer is a reasonable risk. This sweep should include contacting your best sources of leads and any key people you haven't been able to reach lately or who have told you to contact them before accepting an offer.

**Information needed**

You need a great deal of information on a company to make an intelligent decision. Listen carefully in interviews and do some research outside the company. If you must question others, be sensitive and use discretion.

Listed below is a set of items to consider. Not all will be important to you. And you will have information on many of them as a result of your research during your job hunting process. But review those anyway, and from the list select 8 or 10 items that seem most important to you.

1. The job's relationship to your career goals.
2. The job's particular goals and responsibilities and recent history.
3. How the job fits in the total organization—who reports to whom, and so on.
4. Your superior—what problems might arise in working with him or her?
5. Your subordinates—are any problems apparent here?
6. Present management's competence and stability?
7. Company's record during the past five years and its future prospects.
8. Prospects for change in company ownership or control.
9. Company atmosphere—will you be effective and comfortable there?
10. Financial arrangements—salary, frequency of increase, fringe benefits, and so on—are they attractive?
11. Chance for promotion.
12. How the job will affect your life-style and your family—especially if a move is involved.

Information on some items will have to come from people in the company. That on others will result from observation and intuition. However, you can often get some good (and some bad) insight on the company's general reputation from knowledgeable people in the community—bankers, lawyers, stockbrokers, and so on.

Cross-check the answers to such questions as your duties, your reporting relationships, and so on, with a number of key people in the company. If you get different answers from different people, beware.

**Upgrading unsatisfactory offers**

If a company makes you an offer, be realistic and persistent in your search for information and in your negotiations. It's a time when you have maximum leverage, and the higher the job the more opportunity for negotiation.

Your strategy for upgrading offers requires great discretion. An offer may be fair as is—that's ideal. On the other hand, it may be unacceptable because of salary (for example). Try to improve any key aspect of the job *before* you take it if your alternative is to turn it down. As a matter of fact, some companies *expect* you to negotiate.

Offers usually contain some salary slack. Ask for an increase if you feel that is warranted. You may be able to get 5 to 10 percent more. Be careful, though. Pushing too hard for an increase could be a strategic error. You can damage your relationship with the employer so that you are paying for the increase in the long run. Examine the situation carefully.

You might negotiate for an increase in one of two ways: (1) by raising key questions about the conditions surrounding the job, and (2) by widening the scope of the job. In your series of interviews, you may have heard comments that planted questions in your mind about the job (high turnover, new management, long hours, extensive traveling, and so on). If the offer is $50,000 you might say, "I appreciate the offer and I'm very much interested in the job. However, it seems as though you've had a lot of turnover. How secure will my future be even if I do a good job? Also it seems to me that you are having a lot of trouble getting X (a new product) rolling. These are real concerns to me in considering the offer. Frankly, I think I should be getting $56,000."

The second strategy is to negotiate a broadening of job duties. Perhaps you learned that the company is having problems in areas beyond the defined job duties and you might move to broaden them, justifying a higher salary to start (or perhaps later).

If no increase is offered (or if it is unsatisfactory), perhaps you can improve the offer in other ways. Ask when your salary will be reviewed. If the employer says it will be in a year, you might say, "I am very interested in the job, but am quite disappointed in the salary. It would make a lot of difference to me if my first salary review could be at the end of six months." If the company wants you badly enough, this is an easy concession for it to make.

Job security can be a key factor. If it's a high-risk job or requires a move, you might want to negotiate an employment contract. Other alternatives are a termination agreement to protect against abrupt dismissal (your pitch should be to stress the risk of high turnover, and so on). Or you might get the company to guarantee to pay for outplacement counseling if the job doesn't work out.

Other areas for negotiation can be:

1. Promotions (title, responsibilities, becoming a director, committee assignments, timing of promotions).
2. Bonus (try to get a floor under it).

3. Stock options.
4. Pension provisions (such as waiving the waiting period for entry into the plan or shortening the vesting provisions).
5. Vacations.
6. Moving costs being paid for.
7. A company car.
8. Club memberships.
9. Improvements in other fringe benefits.
10. Size of staff.

**Evaluating the offers**

You now have several final offers that are satisfactory. You are ready to evaluate them to make a decision. Prepare a table of your offer(s) using Gordon Sampson's alternative job analysis (Table 3-5). Your first step will be to select the job characteristics to use as measuring sticks from your list of 8 to 10 most important items. Note that some of the factors are facts and others are matters of judgment. How good is your judgment on these items? Can you get more information on them? Which factors are fixed and which are negotiable?

Your next step will be to put these requirements in order. Use the prioritizing tool discussed in Chapter Three, "Who Are You?" and Table 3-3. Now put your analysis aside for a few days.

Next, go through the procedure again as though you were starting from scratch. You may find one or two changes in the list of requirements even at this late date. Compare the requirements used both times and reconcile the differences. Now evaluate your revised requirements as before—list your requirements in priority order and assign a value to each so that the total adds to 100 percent. Write a brief description of your evaluation of each job characteristic for each offer. Then assign the appropriate numerical value for each one for each offer. Total the point values for each offer. Table 12-1 presents an example of this tool.

After you have checked the results, eliminate

**TABLE 12-1**
Alternative jobs analysis (refined), Gordon Sampson

| Job characteristics | Rating | My goal | Numerical value and description | | |
| --- | --- | --- | --- | --- | --- |
| | | | Production manager, ABC Metals | Facilities planning manager, Monarch Co. | Plant superintendent, Foremost Machine |
| The job (responsibilities, title, place in organization) | 18 | Planning—not line | 14. Work I enjoy and do well; lower level than I'd like | 16. Work I enjoy and do well; staff work like this is my strength; report to senior person | 10. Work I like less; is less suited to my interests and strengths; acceptable level in organization |
| Company's status and future prospects | 16 | A well-established company in a strongly growing field | 11. Fair; has had somewhat erratic record; but with some growth; in a very competitive field | 14. Excellent; is known as a very well-run company; consistent growth, preeminent in a strong industry | 7. Poor; company has had weak record in last several years; seems way behind times |
| Company's reputation as a place to work | 14 | Known as fair people; low turnover and few layoffs | 7. Poor; has had quite high turnover; has reputation as being tough people to work for | 12. Very good; low turnover, no real layoffs, known as good place to work | 11. Good; moderate layoffs and turnover |
| Type of boss and close associates | 12 | Prefer high grade professionals who are open and direct | 6. Didn't like 2 of the 5 people I met; liked prospective boss; not really my kind of people | 10. Liked all the people I met; was very favorably impressed by my prospective boss; they're my kind of people | 8. Liked everyone, though several of them didn't seem very professional; quite a bit of nepotism |

| | | $52,000-$55,000 | 9. $50,000 + 5% to 10% bonus | 7. $47,500 + 7% bonus | 10. $51,000 + 5% to 10% bonus |
|---|---|---|---|---|---|
| Starting salary and fringe benefits | 11 | | | | |
| Location | 9 | Don't want to move | 7. No immediate move, possibly one later | 9. No immediate move nor likely in long run | 9. No immediate move nor likely in long run |
| Base to move from (if job fails) | 7 | Broadly needed skills, well respected company | 5. Broadly needed skills in company with mediocre reputation | 4. Very specialized skills in company with excellent reputation | 5. Broadly needed skills in company with fair reputation |
| Personal demands of job (pressure, time demands, traveling) | 6 | Medium pressure, less than 10% traveling; moderate overtime acceptable | 3. Lots of pressure and overtime, little traveling | 3. Medium pressure and overtime; 20% travel | 5. Medium pressure and overtime; no traveling |
| Future salary and fringe benefits | 4 | Good long-term prospects | 3. Moderate risk; good salary increase prospects | 2. Low risk; moderate but steady salary increases | 2. High risk; good salary increase prospects |
| Opportunity for promotion | 3 | Reasonable prospects for promotion | 2. Good chance to become superintendent when he retires in 4 years | 1. Very little chance, but steady growth will increase responsibility of job | 1. Good chance to be manufacturing vice president in 7 years |
| Total | 100 | | 67 | 78 | 68 |

any offers which have total point values much lower than the top two. Compare the numerical ratings for each requirement between the two and revise accordingly. Most likely one offer will continue to be upgraded in your mind, while the other becomes downgraded. This is a good indication of your gut feeling about the jobs—a critical factor in itself. As you go through this process your decision will probably continue to be reinforced, and you will feel more and more comfortable about it.

Personal characteristics are often the key to success on the job (for example, ability to work with people, ability to work independently, being analytically perceptive, etc.). When you have clarified the apparent environment of the job(s), test it against your experience in working in similar types of environment (for example, if your prospective boss is a stickler for detail—how well can you work for such a person?). Focus carefully on your prospective boss. What environment does he or she create? What kind do you work in best? Do they match?

Your analysis of the table can be simplified by using the following questions as a guide:

1. What kind of a person do they really need?
2. How well do I fill this need?
3. What kind of a job do I really need?
4. How well does this job fill this need?

After you have developed your alternative jobs analysis table, get an opinion from several of the people who have most impressed you in your campaign. Their advice can widen your horizons about each job.

**Do you accept a mediocre offer or continue to look?**

Early in your campaign you may get a mediocre offer. What do you do? If you're unable to improve the terms to the point where they become satisfactory, you'll have to make the best decision you can. If you have quite a bit of activity going in your campaign, it probably is a reasonable risk to turn the offer down. There may be one thing worse than being without a job, and that's having a job that doesn't work out after you've been on it a relatively short time.

As time goes on in your campaign, certain people close to you may encourage you to take any job that's offered on the theory that you may not get anything else. Be leery of this. If you accept a mediocre job you may find it very difficult to leave. Also, if you accepted it after a long search, starting all over again will not be easy. It will be hard to get yourself "psyched up" and you will find your friends less responsive to helping you than the first time around. It might seem like you've been out of a job a long time but in a normal 40-year career one or two extra months may be well worth it.

If you're highly marketable, you are especially vulnerable because you may be sought after more than you expected to be. You may have one or several apparently attractive offers made to you before you've really shopped the market. Thus, you may have not had enough time to clarify what you are really looking for. Don't get trapped by this.

**After the decision is made**

After you have accepted an offer and made arrangements to start, you have several other things to do. Turn down any other offers which you have outstanding. Make sure your decision is final, before you do. Err on the side of keeping other offers open until you're absolutely sure everything is right about your first choice.

If you considered other offers carefully and found it difficult to choose one over another, turn them down as delicately as possible. There is the outside chance that you may want to reactivate negotiations with these other companies, perhaps within a few months. In turning offers down, make it clear that you were very favorably impressed by them, that it was a very difficult decision for you, but that you decided on another company.

Once you have accepted your new job, the news may spread rapidly. Make sure you don't tell anyone you've made your final decision until you're ready to have the word get out.

Your final step should be to thank all the key people who helped you in your campaign. You never know when you may need to call on them again.

# Chapter thirteen

# SHOULD YOU MAKE A JOB CHANGE
## (if you have a choice)?

**Myths about job changes**

Up to now we've been concerned with planning and conducting an efficient and effective campaign to locate and then land the job you want. We've assumed that you're unemployed—or about to be—and have to find another job.

Now, suppose that is not the case. Suppose, rather, that, for whatever reason, you want to quit your present job and find another. This chapter explores the factors involved in that situation, beginning with certain myths.

By now you realize that getting a new job involves effort and risk (see Chapter Three under "General Principles"), and that is usually even greater when you're employed. When you have a job, even though it may not be satisfactory, obviously you have the option of staying—something a person unemployed doesn't have. Therefore, as bad as your job may seem, you're giving up something very important.

Moreover, when you're on a job the opportunity for conducting a comprehensive job search doesn't exist. The number of people you can see, the number of offers you can develop, and the opportunity to get the exposure to refine your list of job priorities (and thereby reduce the risk) is extremely limited.

There are a lot of myths about changing jobs. Let's examine some of them:

1. Success in one company means a strong chance of success in a new one.

Though success in one organization seems to follow prior success, there could have been unusually favorable circumstances in the prior one. For example, your success may have been due to the climate within the organization, or you may have brought a specific expertise to the company at the time it was needed. Furthermore, even though a new company may need the changes you can bring about, it may not be willing to pay the required price. In addition, there are numerous instances where a newcomer has effected considerable improvements, but at a price that resulted in superiors not wanting him or her to stay on after the improvements have been achieved.

2. If you've been unsuccessful in one company, you'll probably be better off changing to another.

Such a change works for the better sometimes, but certainly not always. Your lack of success in your current company may be due mainly to you. If you don't correct what's causing it, you're probably not going to achieve what you want in making a change. And you may end up worse!

3. In spite of the odds, *you* will be able to get a better job.

You feel that you are special, and you are. And you may feel that others who didn't make satisfactory changes committed errors you're smart enough to avoid. You may be right—but chances are you're not. Take a realistic look at a cross-section of people you know who've been through a voluntary change and see.

4. You'll make more money.

This is appealing, but how realistic is it? You have undoubtedly heard of people who have made job changes and gotten big increases. It does happen—but much less frequently than you think, particularly at mid-career and beyond. Even if you get it, what will be the real cost? The fact that you'll probably get your next increase at your present company long before your first increase at the new company will offset part of the increment. What is the cost in fringe benefits? If you're well along in your career, you may lose your potential pension. Also you may lose other benefits like the length of vacations, and so on. If a move to another city is involved, will the increase really cover a higher cost of living or moving costs (including the cost of selling your current house and buying a new one) that aren't paid for by your new company? Will a move upset your family?

5. Dissatisfactions with your current job will be corrected in the new one.

This may be true to some extent, but additional dissatisfactions are likely to come up in time. And, in fact, if the key dissatisfactions stem from problems you could have corrected on your current job, you will probably carry them to the new one. And you may well find yourself, after a year on a new job, with a weak power base and in the same doldrums in a brand new company.

6. You're ready for the next promotion but are blocked by a boss who isn't going to move up or retire soon.

This may be true, but it is also true that this situation will change *sometime*. Thus, the real issue is when will it occur? And when it does, will you get the promotion? You probably will get it in your current company in time, if you're doing an outstanding job. If you're not, your chances of making a move to get a job equal to the promotion are limited. So the issue may narrow to timing. Remember the rate of change of personnel in key positions is accelerating. And the changes which can open up the next step in your company can come in one of numerous ways—your boss leaving or retiring, a change in management above him, or an equivalent opportunity elsewhere in the company (say, as a result of an acquisition). In view of these possibilities your best chance may be to wait, and in the meantime to continue to do a good job.

7. You have considerable skill and experience that are not being fully utilized.

That may be. And it is quite possible that you will run into several employers who, if you work hard enough at your job campaign and do a good enough job at it, will hire you for a job that will more fully utilize your skills. But you can be sure that your skills will be looked at in the job market very critically. When you reach mid-career, if you've been successful, the number of jobs are fewer because you are getting close to the top of the organizational pyramid. In addition, we are living in a world where the rapid development of technology is making old skills obsolete at an ever increasing pace. And the number of people competing for good jobs is growing at a rapid rate. For example, roughly double the number of college graduates are employed in 1980 as were employed in 1970.

8. Several companies have expressed interest in you in the past and would be likely to again.

Perhaps. However, if they expressed such interest and you think they may be so attractive, why didn't you accept a job with one of them in the past? What will make those jobs look better today than when you turned them down? There's often a lot more interest in a person when he or she is not available than when a person is.

9. You have never made a major mistake in your career decisions to date so it's unlikely to happen now.

It may be you're in a much better position than most to defy the risks in making a change—and I hope you are, if you decide to do so. But a job change resulting from dissatisfaction with a current position entails a high risk producing similar dissatisfaction. Just as a marriage made on the rebound has a high chance of failure, so does a job change made on an emotional basis.

10. If I don't make a move now, I'll be too old to do it later.

In a working career of 40 years, a year or two really is a pretty small amount of time. Making a move at, say, age 47 isn't really any different than making it at age 45. This is not a time to panic.

11. You have seen lots of executives make mid-career changes, and they seem to be satisfied with them.

It's true, many have made successful changes—some to the best jobs in their lives. But the success of change is much harder to evaluate than it appears to be on the surface. In the first place, a change must be observed over a period of time—probably a five-year minimum. In addition, it is not easy to get any except your closest of friends to reveal their innermost feelings about their jobs. It's only natural that a friend will casually talk about the positive things about his or her job, but how often will someone talk about what may be a very unhappy job when the practical options are limited (and revealing unhappiness may jeopardize the job itself)—and admit that accepting it was a disastrous mistake?

Since 1970, more than 1,000 people have attended the Harvard Business School Alumni Association of Boston job counselling workshop. Over the years approximately 50 percent of the work-shop participants were employed and had the option of staying on their current jobs. Evaluations at the end of each workshop have consistently shown that approximately one half of this group state that the most important thing they learned was the need to go back and take a careful look at their current job again. This is a high percentage.

Because you may be under great emotional stress when you are making the decision about whether to look for another job or not, this may be a good time to use a job counselor. Unfortunately, counselors who are really skilled in helping you to deal with your current emotional pressures and to help you develop skills to improve your performance relatively quickly, are scarce. Guidelines for locating such a counselor are in Chapter Two under "Expecting Real Help from Employment Professionals," "Counselors." In the absence of finding such a person, you may want to talk at length with one or two trusted friends.

You may feel that there is little you can do that would have any real impact on your current situation. That may be true. Or maybe there is much that might be done but isn't obvious. For example, maybe your performance is not what it should be, or you've become discouraged and have just "run out of gas." Maybe things in your life that aren't job related are having a detrimental effect on your job performance and attitude.

Without effective action, your situation is likely to get worse rather than better. Be particularly cautious about leaving a job in an organization with a strong growth record, where "the rising tide lifts all the ships." In such an organization the opportunities for broader responsibilities will increase over time. New jobs at the next-higher level may be created. If the organization is doing poorly, such growth of opportunity is less apparent. However, those who are able to perform well in meeting the company's needs in that kind of a situation have a chance to stand out. All in all, maybe "the devil you know is better than the devil you don't."

**The key is "What do you want to do?"**

You have already been through the step-by-step process to answer the question, "What do you want to do?" if you are actually looking for a job (review Chapter Three). It shows you that if you were unemployed at the time, the initial priority-setting exercise is useful. You would then refine this as you get a better understanding of other opportunities and as your thoughts change with the feedback you get. Since you are employed and not carrying on a campaign at this time, your feedback (to verify your priorities) will be limited—so be conservative in your thinking. For example, it's easy to be overly negative about various aspects of your current job. Try to look at your priorities as a consultant would (for example, someone who wants to discourage you from making a job change). After you have set your priorities, evaluate specifically how your current job measures up against each one of the priorities. Then place a value on each priority, as in Table 12-1. This will be a key way of evaluating specifically the deficiencies in your current job. The next step is a different approach to identify your major frustrations and what you may be able to do about them.

**Reasons for frustration**

Because there are such a variety of reasons (and usually a combination of them) for seriously considering looking for another job, it is important at the outset to identify them. Only then can you work out a program of sensible action. Listed below are most of the reasons executives leave companies voluntarily. Rank each one for its importance to you. Select from the list the three or four most important of these reasons, in your eyes, and then write them down in priority order.

|  | Major factor | Minor factor | No factor at all |
|---|---|---|---|
| 1. You are blocked from promotion . . . | —— | —— | —— |
| 2. You have a personality conflict with your boss . . . . . . . . . . . . . . . . . | —— | —— | —— |
| 3. You feel you can earn more money elsewhere . . . . . . . . . . . . . . . . . | —— | —— | —— |
| 4. You're not being challenged . . . . . . . | —— | —— | —— |
| 5. You've been given poor performance reviews . . . . . . . . . . . . . . . . . . | —— | —— | —— |
| 6. You have a new boss . . . . . . . . . . . | —— | —— | —— |
| 7. You've been offered an unattractive position . . . . . . . . . . . . . . . . . | —— | —— | —— |
| 8. Your division's activity is diminishing . . . . . . . . . . . . . . | —— | —— | —— |
| 9. Your job is one that is not well suited to your particular interests and skills . . . . . . . . . . . . . . . . . | —— | —— | —— |

Now that you have decided the three or four principal reasons for thinking of leaving, let's examine what each of them means for your strategy.

*1. Blocked from promotion.* This could change, for your boss could leave or be moved up, or your duties could be expanded. Furthermore, such changes as an acquisition could improve your role. Another key factor is how interesting and challenging the job is to you. On the other hand, you may have hit your plateau. But, if the prospects are indeed poor for any favorable change in your role within a reasonable time and a promotion is critical for you and you think you're not at the plateau, you'll probably have to move into another place in the company or leave entirely.

*2. Personality conflict.* This is a common situation, and you don't have to be told who wins in a showdown. Don't automatically run away from this kind of situation because it is one that you are likely to meet again. A key factor in your long-term success may be to develop the skill to handle this problem effectively. Once again, if you can't resolve this problem reasonably, and it looks like you will have to live with it for a long time, you'll probably have to make an internal or external move.

*3. More money elsewhere.* Your compensation certainly is a key factor in your job, but it isn't the only one. For the reasons cited in myth number four (see under "Myths about Job Changes" above), unless you are badly underpaid it is quite possible that a move won't bring any substantial improvement for you. Your best opportunity for a *real* increase in your salary, bonus, and so on, may be to improve your performance, and thus your value to the company. Key steps to improve your performance are outlined under "Improving Your Present Job Situation," below.

*4. Lack of challenge.* If you're typical, you like to be challenged, and if you're in a stimulating atmosphere and you have a good boss, you probably are. But many jobs aren't like that. You might have to develop challenges. Try to visualize somebody who is highly motivated and who has just been promoted to your job. How would he or she tackle it? What challenges would another person find in the job? If another could make the job contribute more to the company, your lack of challenge might lie in your attitude and performance. Your best bet to finding challenge is to develop it on your current job. This is an important skill to develop, because what you are experiencing now you may face a number of times in the future. If you don't cope with it successfully, you may meet it again.

*5. Poor performance reviews.* You may feel that these poor reviews are not justified—and you may be right. Whether they are fair evaluations of your work or not, if you can't overcome them you'll probably have to leave. Your only chance of overcoming your frustration from this source is to improve your performance *in your boss's eyes.* This may not mean an actual improvement. It may only mean demonstrating that what you're doing fills your boss's needs.

*6. You have a new boss.* This is often a high-risk situation. The key is how the boss perceives you. If you're seen as someone helpful, you may be safe. This is assuming you can get over any blow to your ego and delay in your career goals. If, on the other hand, you're seen as a threat or an impediment, you may be in trouble. At any rate, you've got nothing to lose by waiting and trying to make the situation work. You can always leave, and sometimes things do change for the better.

*7. You've been offered an unattractive position.* If this doesn't involve relocation, you probably will damage your future in the company by turning it down. So you better accept it and work to make it a constructive step toward your goal. If it doesn't work out, you may still have retained the possibility of making a later move within the company. If the offered job requires relocation, there's less risk—though still some—in turning it down. You'd make a big mistake accepting it if it's strongly opposed by your family. By not relocating, you will retain a stronger base for making a change by staying in a community where you are better known.

*8. Diminished activity.* If the slowdown results from the completion and nonrenewal of a major contract with no move immediately in the offing, your best chance of finding a good job in the company is to anticipate this and try to make a move well before it comes to a head. Otherwise you may find yourself competing with others for a limited number of positions. If it looks as though things will simply be in the doldrums for a while, your estimate of the timing and extent of the recovery is the key. If there is no suitable position within the company, you'll probably have to look outside.

*9. No match between job and interests and skills.* If this is true, you probably will have to find another position. Make sure before you decide to do this, however, that this situation really exists, and that it's not merely rationalization on your part. Your first priority should be to seek another place in your present company where you have a power base.

You have now identified the three or four major frustrations you feel you have about your job. Notice that I have said *you feel.* It is difficult to minimize emotions in making these choices. Visualize how an interested friend would view these choices and consider if he or she would substitute one or more other choices instead. Using this approach, make your final choice of the most realistic reasons. Having done this, now let's see what some of your options are in coping with them.

**Biting the bullet**

Your first alternative is to stay on your present job, doing it day-to-day as you have been. In view of the frustrations that prompted you to consider leaving it, your chances of finding real satisfaction, doing it as you are now, are slight. You are also guaranteeing that you'll get little satisfaction from your job. True, some people gain their satisfaction by getting deeply engrossed in outside interests. However, you certainly recognize that more than half of your discretionary time is spent on the job

or commuting to and from it. Of the 168 hours in
the week, sleeping, eating, dressing, and so on, ac-
count for roughly 68 hours—activities you'd be
doing regardless of what your job is. The normal
work week for most of us is a minimum of 50
hours, if you include commuting time, and probably a lot longer. So time for outside activity is
short in any case. Looking at the more positive
side—with perhaps a real effort on your part, you
might greatly increase job satisfaction by improving your present job situation or by changing jobs
within your present company.

**Improving your**
**present job**
**situation**

A key reason for staying, at least for a while, is
to see if you can work things out to your satisfaction. This can carry over, for there probably will be
several times in the future when things aren't going
right on your job. Having developed the skill to
adapt to your situation and make of it what you
want may be even more important then than now.
So let's take a look at some general approaches to
improving your job situation.

A key to having a satisfying job is gaining the
recognition and support of the political powers
that affect your job. It is therefore important that
you understand your job's political environment
and learn how to handle it effectively.

At the start I want to emphasize that this process is playing politics *effectively* and not in a
vicious or self-promoting way. Company politics
has all kinds of nasty connotations, mostly given it
by people who don't understand it or who don't
cope well with it. At one extreme is the *knifer-in-*
*back.* He or she soon develops such an antagonism
within the organization that it becomes self-defeat-
ing. And the other extreme is the *avoider.* This is
the individual who carefully skirts becoming
involved, usually to his or her own detriment. In
the middle is the effective executive who knows

how to read the political chemistry of an organization and how to handle him/herself to get the job done as well as possible within it. There is nothing wrong or immoral in this. The person is merely realistic and sensitive to how key people react in roles that greatly affect his or her work.

Knowing who has the power is a key. Part of this results from the formal organization (the organization chart) and part is from the *informal* organization (the actual relationships that exist because of the individuals involved). To understand the informal relationships you must be observant. What roles do people really play? Who has the power in what committees? Who eats lunch regularly with whom? Who is involved in outside activities (for example, socializes, plays golf, and so on) with whom? They result from a variety of different things such as key individuals' information pipelines, seniority, personality, personal relationships (old friends, relatives, and the like).

If you later choose to look for another job outside, you will find you have a crucial need for evaluating the political relationships in any new organization you're considering. Believe me, it is difficult to evaluate this structure within a company in the course of perhaps only three or four interviews for a new job. Thus, a key factor in your future success will be the improvement of your skill in identifying the political relationships in your work environment and improving your effectiveness in working with them.

In evaluating the politics of your work environment, here are some key questions for you: What kinds of people are my bosses? What are their backgrounds? What are their personal goals? How do they live? What are their biases? Religious, social, and ethnic backgrounds can be terribly important. If you are in a company of WASPS and you're not one, your chances of long-term success can be quite limited. Answers to some of these are easy to get but others come only through observing and listening.

After you've identified the powerholders and learned what kind of people they are, you have to ask yourself a key question. Can you reasonably expect their support? If you cannot as you are currently behaving, is it reasonable to expect you can change enough to win their support? If it is unreasonable, should you decide to look elsewhere, or accept your current situation and prospects?

We have already seen that a key to your success is how your boss, say, Jack Barnes, feels about you. So you must understand the role that Barnes plays. In this evaluation consider not only your boss, but (depending on the organization) the surrounding hierarchy (Barnes's boss, influential peers, and so on). But the primary focus will be on your boss. Answer carefully the following questions:

What is expected of Barnes (for example, job requirements, the pressures to perform)?

What are his personal goals?

What are his basic biases?

Answer these questions to yourself in writing. Basic to Barnes's feelings about you are how you help him do what's expected of him and what he wants done. Understanding his job requirements, his personal goals, and his personal biases will enable you to better grasp why he behaves the way he does. It may be that you don't like or agree with some of the things you identify. That will probably be the case. These are things you'll have to accept if you want to develop a more satisfactory relationship with him. It is desirable to get this understanding before you evaluate how he rates your performance.

Next fill out your best estimate of how Barnes would rate your performance (Table 13-1). A grade of C is considered satisfactory. What are the rea-

**TABLE 13-1**
Rating your performance versus your peers* (as Jack Barnes would rate you)

|  | A | B | C | D | E |
|---|---|---|---|---|---|
| Your overall job performance? . . . . . . . . . . . | ___ | ___ | ___ | ___ | ___ |
| How well do you do what Barnes wants? . . . . . | ___ | ___ | ___ | ___ | ___ |
| Do you help him achieve his personal goals? . . . | ___ | ___ | ___ | ___ | ___ |
| Do you help him do his job better? . . . . . . . . | ___ | ___ | ___ | ___ | ___ |
| Are you sensitive to his biases? . . . . . . . . . . | ___ | ___ | ___ | ___ | ___ |
| Do you communicate effectively with him? . . . | ___ | ___ | ___ | ___ | ___ |
| Do you ever embarrass him? . . . . . . . . . . . . | ___ | ___ | ___ | ___ | ___ |
| How loyal are you to him? . . . . . . . . . . . . . | ___ | ___ | ___ | ___ | ___ |
| Is he proud to have you on his team? . . . . . . . | ___ | ___ | ___ | ___ | ___ |
| How well does your background fit the image of what he would like you to be? . . . . . . . . | ___ | ___ | ___ | ___ | ___ |
| How well would he rate you as his representative to others? . . . . . . . . . . . . | ___ | ___ | ___ | ___ | ___ |
| Do you make a difference in the operation? . . . | ___ | ___ | ___ | ___ | ___ |
| How well do you set priorities and work toward them? . . . . . . . . . . . . . . . . . . | ___ | ___ | ___ | ___ | ___ |
| Do you anticipate your boss's needs? . . . . . . . | ___ | ___ | ___ | ___ | ___ |
| Do you only put out fires or do you anticipate? . . . . . . . . . . . . . . . . . . . | ___ | ___ | ___ | ___ | ___ |
| How much effective work do you produce? . . . | ___ | ___ | ___ | ___ | ___ |
| Do you frequently get too much involved in detail? . . . . . . . . . . . . . . . . . . . . | ___ | ___ | ___ | ___ | ___ |
| What is the quality of your work? . . . . . . . . . | ___ | ___ | ___ | ___ | ___ |
| How well motivated are you? . . . . . . . . . . . . | ___ | ___ | ___ | ___ | ___ |
| How well do you meet deadlines? . . . . . . . . . | ___ | ___ | ___ | ___ | ___ |
| How well do you communicate? . . . . . . . . . . | ___ | ___ | ___ | ___ | ___ |
| Are you effective in leading meetings? . . . . . . | ___ | ___ | ___ | ___ | ___ |
| Are you effective in participating in meetings? . . . . . . . . . . . . . . . . . . . . | ___ | ___ | ___ | ___ | ___ |

TABLE 13-1 *(continued)*

|                                                    | A | B | C | D | E |
|----------------------------------------------------|---|---|---|---|---|
| Are you effective in developing people? . . . . . . | ___ | ___ | ___ | ___ | ___ |
| Are you a team player? . . . . . . . . . . . . . . . | ___ | ___ | ___ | ___ | ___ |
| Are you resourceful in solving problems? . . . . . | ___ | ___ | ___ | ___ | ___ |
| How promotable are you? . . . . . . . . . . . . . . | ___ | ___ | ___ | ___ | ___ |
| Are you easy to work for? . . . . . . . . . . . . . | ___ | ___ | ___ | ___ | ___ |
| How well do you anticipate future trends? . . . . | ___ | ___ | ___ | ___ | ___ |
| How much are you doing to broaden your vision? . . . . . . . . . . . . . . . . . . . . . . . | ___ | ___ | ___ | ___ | ___ |

*Your boss's other subordinates.

sons for any D or E grades? If Barnes's job opened up, would you get it? If not, why not? Answers to these questions will give you a pretty good idea of how you stand in your boss's eyes.

The marks you give yourself while pretending to be Barnes should identify strengths and weaknesses. It's hard to develop a program to do something about the latter, but even so it may be easier than getting a better job elsewhere. The keys to such a program are summed up by:

1. Do better work.
2. Present a more favorable image.

The first step will be a program to overcome the deficiencies revealed in your performance rating. Let's say that through this checklist you pinpoint your major deficiencies in meeting Barnes's level of performance as:

Not helping him do his job better.
Not keeping him well informed.
Not setting priorities and working toward them.
Not anticipating Barnes's needs.
Not meeting deadlines.

Prepare a "report card" of these items. At the end of each day take five minutes to rate yourself on how well you did on each of these items, using a scale of A to E. Any day that you have a grade of D or lower on any of these items, write down a list of the things that you are going to do *tomorrow* to improve the grade on each item.

The "Dialogue Tool" can work here. Visualize yourself conducting a conversation with an imagined consultant on why you performed poorly on a particular day. For example, on "How do you meet deadlines?" you got a grade of D.

---

| *Consultant* | *You* |
|---|---|
| Why did you get a *D*? | I didn't complete the recommendation on the revision of the next quarter's department budget until 3 o'clock. My secretary had to stop everything to type it in preparation for the 3:30 meeting. Also because I was rushed, I didn't do as good research on the excess overtime as I would have liked. |
| Why didn't you start on the project sooner? | I was busy working on the new system for computerizing the inventory. |
| When did you know you had to revise the budget? | After the last monthly meeting on February 15. |
| When did you start on the budget revision? | A week ago—March 7. Then Harry was away for three days so I couldn't get the information I needed from him until yesterday. |
| Do you mean to say you didn't have any time between 2/15 and 3/7 to get the budget? | No, but other more important things seemed to interfere. |
| Based on this experience, if you had a chance to do it over again, what would you do? | Get started on 2/15. |

| *Consultant* | *You* |
|---|---|
| Were there resources available you didn't use? Could you have delegated more of it? | Yes, Bill could have been assigned to an analysis of the overtime. |
| Do you have other projects right now you may be facing a deadline on? | Yes, the inventory systems computerization is due 3/22 and the revision of the cost reports 3/27. |
| What can you *do tomorrow* to make sure you'll avoid the schedule crunch on these? | Set up a schedule for the key steps on each project.* |
| Is there anything else? | Can delegate part of the inventory system to Mary* |
| What if Barnes assigns you another hot project like preparing his report for the division manager's meeting. You know it took almost two days last month. What would you wish you had done tomorrow? | Pulled Tom off the new cost report revision and assigned him to the inventory project.* |

*Items to go on your report card for tomorrow.

The dialogue technique is a means of forcing you to extend yourself to use more resources than you otherwise might. In it, your consultant is the *heavy* to force you to think more deeply than you ordinarily would. It's important that you do it in writing—otherwise, your mind glosses over things that probably won't even be addressed. This example is unusually long to give you an in-depth understanding of the use of the tool. You'll learn with practice to write out the key items in notes—with the same effect as spelling them out in complete sentences. As action items are completed, remove them from your report card. Also remove your weaknesses from the list as you feel you have them under control.

A second key to improving performance is making sure that you are devoting enough time to your highest-priority projects. A recent subscription promotion of *Business Week* made the following statement: "Studies have shown that most people spend 80% of their time on the least important 20% of their jobs . . . and only 20% of their time on work which yields 80% of the bottom-line results." A key tool is learning to work the 20/80 percent rule.

Your first step is to evaluate how you are spending your time now. For a one- or two-week period keep track in 15-minute increments of how you spend each day. How much of your time went to things you have no control over? In tabulating this category, be sure that in fact you did have no control. Were there things on this list that you got involved in unnecessarily or could have handled in some other way (for example, had a subordinate represent you)?

You want to focus particularly on your discretionary time. Some of that time is in *maintenance* work—routine things necessary to keep your operation going (meeting with your staff, supervising them on projects, correspondence, and so on). Analyze each of these items. Is it necessary for you to be involved in all of them? Looking at each after the fact, knowing what you know now, was there some way you could have got it done using less of your time? Have you allowed people around you to get in the habit of *delegating upward* (that is, dumping on you things they should be doing themselves)?

The balance of your discretionary time is truly discretionary. This is the time, if used effectively, that can have the biggest payoff for you. Was each item in the 20 percent with the highest payoff or the 80 percent with the lowest payoff? What should you do differently in the future so that a much greater part of this time is spent on the projects in the 20 percent with the highest chance of payoff?

Your work has fallen in a pattern—partly from habits developed over 15, 20, or 25 years. Part of this pattern results from the work habits of your subordinates. It is no easy task to break these. Visualize a new, tough, and resourceful boss taking over your job. Wouldn't Barnes, for example, quickly get these patterns changed to get what he wants done—or else? The most effective payoff for you may be in changing your work patterns, and engineering the changes you would like to see in those you should depend on most.

You have already seen how to use the "Failure Analysis Tool" in planning time in your campaign (see Chapter Eleven). Plan your time on the job in exactly the same way. For example, take five minutes at the start of the day to ask yourself, "If I fail to get done today what I should, what will the likely reasons be and what would I wish I had done differently?" Visualize yourself at the end of the day—what are the things that would most upset you if they weren't completed? What different actions might you have taken? Using a few minutes to write down these items and outlining the action you want to take will force you to develop a list of priorities for today. The thrust of your efforts is to work toward the highest-priority items on your list, adding new priority items as they come up. Add to your daily report card the key assignments you planned to accomplish during the day. Rate your performance on them the same way you rate your deficiencies.

If you force yourself to use this report-card approach and dialogue your D's and E's daily, you can make substantial strides to correct some of these deficiencies. By doing this you are using tools to improve your own performance that are similar to those you as a good executive use for correcting any problems of your company that fall within your jurisdiction.

An additional source of ideas for improving your performance is what you can learn from *superstars* (those whose performance you admire—either in your current company or those you've known in prior companies). If you are facing a tough problem, what would one of them probably do to solve it? If you are dissatisfied with a job you've done, ask yourself what your superstar would have done differently.

The best prepared plans often aren't carried out to achieve the results wanted. Yours often won't be either. To refine your daily evaluation of performance, provide the motivation to make the tool work. There are two ways to accomplish this. First, you can reduce the time period for evaluation—to half a day or even an hour. For example, let's say you had five "must" jobs to do yesterday and accomplished only three of them. Today you have six in this category. Decide on the high priority ones you can reasonably expect to do in the morning. Evaluate your success on them just before lunch. Adjust your afternoon schedule accordingly.

This tightening of the periods for evaluation soon becomes cumbersome—so you want to stretch it out to, say a day, as soon as you're making progress again. Second, you can invoke a penalty or penalties for poor performance. Such penalties could be such things as staying late, coming in Saturday, taking work home, giving up lunch with a friend or your morning coffee break. The penalty is most effective when it is related to your deficiency (for example, to give up your favorite TV program to work on a missed assignment). Increasing self-discipline forces you to make greater efforts and to be more resourceful in working on your high priorities.

The third part of your approach to improve your performance is to carry out a program of improvement projects that will get high priority things done (that is, projects in the 80 percent pay-off category). These will be your *showcase* projects. Before you put a lot of time into any one of them, you might test the general idea of each in a low-key way with your boss to make sure you don't put a lot of work into something that he or she has little interest in.

The one or two most desirable showcase projects should have top priority on your discretionary time on the job. The action needed on these projects should also be added to your daily report card. As much as possible, these projects should be ones that will make your boss look good. Not only should such projects be carried out well, but it is important that they be communicated discreetly to those individuals who have most jurisdiction over your future.

A fourth area for improvement is your conduct in meetings. A major portion of our business lives is spent in meetings, from formal, regular committee meetings to informal meetings with one or two people working on specific problems. A key to favorable evaluation of your performance is in how well you conduct yourself in meetings, particularly those involved with your boss. If you feel you are not performing well in them, there are certain things that you can do to improve.

One means is to define the ways you are not an effective committee member. Are you improperly prepared? Do you frequently lack information you should have at your fingertips? Are you weak in contributing to thinking which is accepted and acted upon? Do you take controversial stands that antagonize the most powerful committee members?

Having identified your deficiencies, you should take some time to prepare for each important meeting to minimize them. At the start it will be important to take more time than you may think necessary to prepare, but as your performance improves, the time for preparation should decrease substantially. Right after each meeting you should make a quick analysis of your performance. How did you rate overall? What were the items you were not prepared for? Why weren't you prepared? If your performance in the meeting didn't help to a reasonable extent in arriving at the decision, why didn't it? Knowing what you know about the meeting, what do you wish you had done differently? What will you do differently next time? It may be that if you have not been an active participant in the meetings, you will want to develop several questions or key points before each meeting to interject at the appropriate time, so you'll start to build up a greater level of participation. Have them written out and in front of you at each meeting and check each off as it comes up.

Perhaps you come out of many meetings feeling "That solution was obvious. Why couldn't I have come up with it?" Or maybe your reaction is "I don't agree with the decision. Why didn't they consider thus and so?" Your post-meeting analysis should go along the lines of "Why didn't I think of thus and so in the meeting?" or, "Why didn't I prevent it?" "What am I going to have to do before the next meeting, so I don't miss a similar opportunity?" Preparing a checklist for each meeting, based on your prior meeting evaluations and the topics expected to be discussed, will be very helpful.

Still another way to improve performance is to step up your motivation. This is not an easy thing to do unless you are spurred to action. Maybe you have become complacent in your job. You may also feel that it is quite secure. See if the following scenario will shake you out of this frame of mind.

It's the middle of Friday afternoon and the phone rings. Your secretary gives you the message that your boss, Paul Travers, wants you to come up to his office right away. After he has asked you to sit down and you have exchanged a few pleasantries, Travers says: "Harry, I'm afraid I've got some bad news for you. You know we have been undergoing quite a change here at XYZ. You also know that I told you several times in the last year or so that your performance wasn't really measuring up. I'm well aware that you have been here a long time and have made quite a few contributions to the company over the years. Unfortunately things change—and they've changed a lot here. To be perfectly frank there is no place for you here in this picture. Therefore, I am telling you that you are being let go as of today. This decision is final. I have discussed this several times with JB [the president] and he agrees. I'm very sorry it has come to this but it may be the best thing for you in the long run. To help you in this transition, we are going . . . ."

If your motivation hasn't been the strongest, think of this scenario coming to pass. It may be much closer to reality than you think.

The final thing to improve your job situation is to see what adjustments can be made in the non-job-related aspects of it. It may be that you have got into a rut in these aspects of your life and are not getting the satisfaction out of them that you might. This may be having an adverse effect on your job performance. Or maybe significant changes have taken place in your life in recent years that are making it less satisfying. Provided it does not infringe on the demands of your job, this may be a good time to get involved in something in your community or in a hobby that you have always wanted to pursue. Such things can add a dimension to your life that can be very rewarding, and indirectly make your job situation more satisfactory.

Don't expect this kind of self-improvement program to bring about great results overnight, but over a period of six months or a year it can considerably improve things for you.

You have nothing to lose by making an intensive effort to improve performance on your current job; you may have a lot to gain by it. Most of all you can considerably improve your management skills. Effective self-improvement can give you key tools that will be valuable for the rest of your career. Achieving your career goals in your present job may well be the preferred solution. If ultimately you decide to make a job search outside the company, these improved skills can help your effectiveness in this search and ultimately on the new job. This is a time to consider seeking a counselor to help you implement your program.

**Get another job in your company**

We have already seen how an effective outplacement program can help you conduct a more effective job campaign by clarifying your objectives and identifying your most marketable experiences, and finally improving your ability to sell yourself. One of the larger and more reputable outplacement firms has discovered an interesting phenomenon. That group's experience shows that upon the completion of their outplacement program, about 10 percent of the clients end up accepting jobs with the same company that recently fired them. Furthermore, in roughly half of the cases these individuals have ended with more responsible jobs and higher salaries. This fact shows the effectiveness of an outplacement program in identifying clients' skills and goals and improving their ability to sell themselves. It also indicates that many executives, when they effectively present themselves to the right people, can be offered other jobs within their companies. Therefore, if you decide that you want to change from your current job, you should first ask: "Is there another job within the company that would satisfy my needs?" Obviously in a great many instances such a career change within the company is not possible. But if you have identified the particular area in your company you are interested in, try to develop the most favorable image of yourself with the key person there. At an appropriate time make your interest known. You probably will have to be patient, but if you've made a favorable impression an offer may be forthcoming in time.

If you are interested in making a substantial shift of careers (for example, from production to sales), it is particularly desirable to do it within your company. In fact, it may be easier to do it in your current company than outside. And if this change doesn't work out, you have a much better chance to move into another job within the company. This is far less risky than trying to make this transition to a new career in a new company.

**How to leave your company**    If you have decided definitely to leave your company first ask yourself this question, "Should I resign or should I wait until I have found another job?" If you wait, you really don't have much to lose. Rarely are you better off to resign.

In resolving this question, remember that getting another job probably will not be easy and that the best approach is first to try and locate a job while you're still working. One advantage here is that you are more attractive to prospective employers if you are still working. For example, executive recruiters are very leery of recommending job hunters who are out of work to their clients. In fact, only about 5 percent of the people hired through executive recruiting efforts are out of work. Another reason for remaining on the job while you are looking is that you are maximizing your options. Changes may occur within the company that make it more desirable for you to stay.

On the negative side, however, conducting a job search while you are on the job is likely to expose you to only a few job possibilities. You will also have only a limited amount of time to carry on a campaign. And your campaign may be discovered.

If you decide to stay on the job while you are conducting your job search, your campaign strategy depends on the company environment and your relationship with your boss. If it is a good relationship, your boss may let you search to a limited extent while you are on the job. In fact, some bosses encourage it, because they feel that sometimes an employee, when exposed to the realities of the market outside, comes to realize that the old job is better than he or she thought and as a result tackles it with new vigor.

If your relationship with your boss makes it unlikely that he or she would approve of your search, you must carry on a confidential campaign. The first step in this, and it is often not considered carefully, is to undergo the same sort of intensive preparation that is outlined in this book for someone who is out of work. This probably will take a lot of self-control, because the kind of preparation which is emphasized here may require you to drag out the start of your search for such a long time that you may get impatient and decide impulsively to make contacts with employers and agencies before you are effectively prepared. Often this is the downfall of a good confidential campaign.

Once adequately prepared, start your campaign with a limited number of contacts (your closest friends in influential positions plus a few selected executive recruiters). Once you have made your first contact, you have introduced a risk that could put your job in jeopardy. It is difficult for you to know just what relationship each contact might have with your boss or another key person in your organization. There are three things to do at this stage. First, be very selective about these contacts. Second, make clear to them that this is a confidential campaign. Third, and this is often the key to a confidential campaign, be patient—it is not unusual for a confidential campaign to take 12 months or more. Also prepare yourself for the possibility that your boss will discover that you are looking. This could be catastrophic, but it may be just awkward. What is likely to happen here again depends on your company and the type of boss you have, and your relationship with him or her. You may be asked to leave immediately (even with no severance pay in spite of long service) or a limit may be placed on the time you can take off and a deadline set for your leaving, or you may be encouraged to stay. If you want to preserve your option to stay, there are several approaches you might take. None guarantees success, but they may be worth a try. For example:

You can deny that you've been looking (but it's unlikely you'll get away with it). Or you could say:

"I was approached, and while it's very unlikely I'd be interested, I could see little harm in listening to what the possibility was."

"I did casually check out this one possibility that I was approached on and I decided my situation is much better here—so I turned it down and intend to stay."

"I have been looking and hope you'll give me some time to work things out."

"Every few years during my career, for my own long-term career plan, I've felt I should casually check out the market—as it is very hard to get a perspective on my progress otherwise."

At any rate, you should be prepared to be asked to leave and ready to move your campaign into high gear if it happens.

If you're looking for another job, a key decision is your strategy. Many people make the decision to leave primarily because they are looking for more money. The desire to earn more money is natural, but it can lead you into a trap of taking a job which is not really a good one for your career in the long run. That is not to say that money is not important. But even more important than your immediate pay is the type of job experience you will be getting and the long-range possibilities (and future pay) of the job. If these two priorities are met satisfactorily, your desire to earn more money will be satisfied in time.

Another important consideration on leaving your job is timing. In a period of recession, a great many organizations are in difficulty. Ordinarily this is a poor time to leave voluntarily, because few jobs are available and an unusually large number of people are looking for them. So put all your energies into improving your performance on the job— so that when the job market does become more favorable, you will have improved your credentials for making a desirable switch.

A final thought on quitting—make sure that when you walk out the door for the last time, you leave the most favorable impression possible. Some individuals have become so frustrated with their situation that they proceed to tell their boss and other key people in the company off. There is nothing to gain by doing this—other than giving yourself *temporary* personal satisfaction. On the other hand, you may have a lot to lose in terms of getting favorable references from your company. Furthermore, acting so immaturely can cause a feeling of guilt which may act as a considerable drag at a critical time (when you're conducting a job campaign).

**When approached by an executive recruiter**

Some day you may receive a call from an executive recruiter. To find good candidates for their assignments, they often phone key people in their clients' industries for recommendation of candidates. Such a call often is to discover whether or not the individual called might be interested, although the implication may not be there at all.

Invariably these calls come to your office. If you're interested, ask for a phone number so that you can call back privately. You would think that executive recruiters, to be effective, would respect confidentiality. Any reputable one will, but not all do. Do not run the risk. Ask for a description of the job and say you'd like to think of candidates and call him back. You might casually ask the names of any people the recruiter has worked with whom you might know—so you can check his or her reputation as a protection for yourself or anyone you might recommend. In considering whether you are seriously interested in pursuing the possibility, first recognize that it can be flattering to be approached by an executive recruiter—there aren't many things more flattering than having someone indicate a desire to hire you.

**When approached by another company**

Here is a situation that is similar to some extent to being approached by an executive recruiter, but in this instance there is a somewhat better prospect of an offer. Whether you consider this approach seriously depends on how attractive it sounds and the risks involved. If you decide to pursue it, evaluate the possibility in terms of your job and the financial and personal priorities versus your current job. Following the procedures outlined in Chapter Three, What Do You Want to Do? and

Chapter Twelve, Making the Decision, should help here. In measuring your current job, remember the risks of making a change and the unrealized potential in your current job (viz the early part of this chapter).

# Chapter fourteen

# STRATEGIES FOR SPECIFIC BACKGROUNDS

**General principles**

You now have the general principles for preparing and executing a job campaign. But if you're like most job hunters, you feel that you have certain unique drawbacks because of your background and what you are trying to achieve, and for some people, these drawbacks are very real. Even so, there are certain strategies for tailor-making the whole job-search process to overcome a major difficulty such as being older, wanting to shift from government to industry, or changing careers. This chapter deals with how to adapt the principles you have learned so far to your particular situation. The most common of these drawbacks will be dealt with in some depth, while the less common will be touched on briefly. Look at the headings below to see if any of these apply to you.

The older job hunter.

Government to industry.

Changing careers.

The job hopper.

A physical or emotional disability.

Out of work for a long time.

Lack of experience in your chosen field.

A confidential campaign.

Poor recent experience.

Lacking in-depth experience of your peers.

A mixed background.

A move to another location.

Specialist in a declining industry.

Downgrading yourself.

Expert in a small, highly specialized industry.

Remember the following guidelines apply whether or not you have any of these drawbacks:

1. In dealing with employers make sure that your favorable experiences and skills are emphasized both in your resume and in interviews. Recognize employers are always looking for strong candidates. Find out what they feel constitutes such a candidate. Then present your credentials so they appear to meet these desired requirements as closely as possible.
2. Try to play down your deficiencies as much as possible.
3. Recognize that employers are often going to put the spotlight on them, and develop a positive strategy to deal with any that apply to you. For example, if you are older, you have the positive advantage of more years of experience plus maturity and stability, compared to someone younger.
4. Expend your main efforts on employers who have historically hired individuals such as yourself. For example, older workers have in general had much better success in approaching smaller, less talent-laden organizations.

**The older
job hunter**

If you're in your 50s or your early 60s, you may feel that you have an insurmountable problem. There is no question that there are real difficuities, but they can be overcome. Many people at your age have landed excellent jobs—some even the best jobs in their lives. I have seen a number of them do this. There's no question that the jobs are fewer, that you may have to work harder to get the one you want, and perhaps make greater compromises— but there's a good job there for you if you put on an effective campaign and are patient.

Your best prospects are situations where you'll be hired by someone of like age or older—unless your skills are in a field that's in short supply. To younger prospective bosses, there's no way that you are really going to hide your general age bracket. What you must do is develop your approach to overcome the stereotype of the older worker as being inflexible, unmotivated, and even tired. This is a classic case where you may be turned down because of "unasked questions." Aggressively make points to overcome this unfavorable image.

Convey that you are a vigorous person by stressing the long hours you have worked in recent years and citing any demanding athletic or outdoor activities that you have engaged in. Convey a high degree of motivation by showing challenges you have dealt with in recent years. Stress your flexibility. Show your ability to listen perceptively and ask intelligent questions. Show that you have the ability to get to the heart of a problem and can select a solution that has reasonable flexibility. Try to get across experience that shows your skills are up-to-date and that you can work for (or with) younger workers.

Don't let your appearance work against you. At a minimum get outside every day for a long walk. Also get plenty of rest. Dressing in clothes that people in their late 30s and early 40s wear may help you. As suggested earlier, stress your experience, your maturity, and your stability. If you have worked successfully for a younger man, say so. In your resume, you may want to omit your college dates and perhaps the earliest years of your career.

**Government to industry**

Don't let anybody tell you that experience in government isn't useful to industry, if it is marketed properly. There are loads of examples of career government-service people, particularly military ones, who have made the transition very successfully.

You do have several hurdles to overcome though. Government is often thought of by industry as inefficient and not profit conscious. You need to stress your successful experience in the kinds of things that industry needs—such as making cost savings, meeting time and budget goals, and innovation. Civilians often think that things are achieved in the military, for example, only by giving orders. Show examples of how you accomplished things the same way as in the business world—by planning with your associates, getting their cooperation, and then carefully overseeing the execution of the plan.

Many making the transition from government to industry have difficulty in describing their experience in business rather than in government terms. "Take off the uniform in your terminology, and dress it in civilian clothes." Former government employees who have made this transition successfully could be a big help to you on this. If such a person is not available, you may want to interview, for information only, a number of people in your chosen field until you understand what they typically are looking for and some of the terminology that they use. Hiring a part-time consultant could be useful. The resume of Francis L. Townsend

(Resume 6-10 in Chapter Six) shows you a way to describe military experience in civilian terms.

Some civilian employers may think that you are looking for a job in industry just to supplement a high government pension, and therefore lack the kind of motivation they are looking for. Stress here that you are really looking for a challenge, and cite experience that shows how you have coped successfully with major problems.

Particularly look for companies and activities most like your government experience or where your experience is an asset (i.e., the defense industry). Your search may also be eased if you get away from areas where there is a heavy concentration of government jobs (Washington, D.C., near military bases, and so on).

## Changing careers

You may have had 10 or 15 years of production experience, for example, and want to get into finance. Make sure that the career you're shooting for isn't just a pipe dream. The grass *isn't* always greener on the other side of the street. Your first step is to understand the real requirements of the job that you're shooting for and what it would be like to have that kind of a role day after day. This step should answer the question of whether or not the new field would be right for you. It should also help you get a better understanding of the requirements of the job. Your second step is to make an in-depth analysis of what you've done—from which should come a pattern of the things that you really like to do and do most effectively. Being able to point to experience in your own field that has comparability to your desired field can be a real plus for you. It will be helpful to review the section in the Gordon Sampson example dealing with making your career decision (see Chapter Three). In order to make a convincing case for yourself, you must show that you have developed strong skills in your other experience that will be useful in a new career.

Many people will wonder how strong a conviction you have about the new field. A long and successful record in another field may help allay their fears. You should be aware that a search for a different career may take longer and mean a reduction in your immediate salary. Some people in the new field will discourage you because they are overly protective of their own image and they pride themselves on the difficulty of attaining the position that they're in. It may be helpful to cite people in your chosen field who have made the transition from other jobs. Finally, if you have a job now, try to make the career change in your present company, because if you've had a good record and the new job doesn't work out you may find an opportunity to move back into your old field or into a third field in the company. This may take real patience, but it may be more than made up for by knowing the company and the people involved, and having a power base in it.

A key tool in your strategy for changing careers is your resume. A typical chronological resume emphasizes experience in your own field and immediately makes you a poor candidate for a job in a new field. So develop a functional resume. A good example is that of Frank J. Harrison (Resume 6-2).

**The job hopper**     Murray Foster was an excellent job hunter. He had the record to prove it. Ten jobs in the last 10 years. Murray's problem was that he was an expert at finding unsuitable jobs. If this is your problem, the key to it is your poor choice of jobs. Whenever anybody shows any interest in you for a job, do you jump at it? This same characteristic also serves you poorly on the job, because when things go wrong you may avoid facing up to them and, either by your own choice or the employer's, the job doesn't work out. If this characteristic is deep-seated, seek out a counselor; for example, a psychologist who will work with you to overcome it. Your record has shown an ability to get jobs, so use this skill to its fullest in your new campaign, but be persevering in trying to get a really suitable offer.

Structure your resume to minimize your erratic job record, and to play up your successes on your jobs. Murray Foster's original resume was chronological and listed the 10 jobs he held in the last 10 years on the first page. In what more blatant way could he advertise the fact that he had an unstable work record? A functional resume, such as Natalie Arhanian's (Resume 6-12), deemphasizes her unstable job record and plays up the positive experience she has had. A reader of it is impressed immediately by Arhanian's accomplishments and may be less critical of her unstable work record.

If you have been a job hopper because of your impulsiveness, it is particularly important that you follow the cardinal rule that you get three *good* job offers. The fact that you have demonstrated ability to get jobs proves that you can do it. A key part of your strategy is outlined in Chapter Twelve. Stalling will allow you to buy the time necessary to get a second and third good offer. From these three good offers, you should be able to make an intelligent decision on the one that best suits your long-term goals and interests.

Accepting the job is the first step. The experience of having developed the patience to get three good job offers will have developed in you an improved skill in keeping your impulsiveness in check. You will need this perseverance even more on the job if you want to make it an enduring one. This should be a prime goal of your self-development program. If something comes up that really bothers you, discipline yourself to say nothing or do nothing that can have an adverse effect on relationships with the people you work with. You probably will have to greatly overcompensate for this tendency until you get it under control.

**A physical or emotional disability**

You may have a hearing problem or a stammer or another physical disability. You may find that getting a job is more difficult than it is for most people. On the other hand, you can look around your community and find others with your same affliction who are employed. If you approach somebody who has a similar difficulty in the right way, that person will probably be more willing to see you and perhaps steer you to resources that might be useful. A key factor in your job search is to have a realistic goal.

Use any available agency that deals with people with your disability. Such an agency will have the most competent counseling, or know of it, and will know of employers who are most responsive to someone like you. Remember, agencies are usually understaffed and have limited resources, but regardless of this they are probably your best bet as a source of help.

A key factor in dealing with employers is making clear to them what you can and cannot do. Those who have had few dealings with a disabled person probably will overemphasize the negative effects of disability. Therefore, it is important that you play up strongly the kinds of things that you have done. And your best chances are with employers that have a reputation for hiring disabled people or with smaller and nonprofit organizations. Many of the latter have a need for management skills and have more flexible hiring standards. The same is true of people with emotional problems.

**Out of work for a long time**

Because of illness or family problems you may not have been able to work for a long time, say a year or more. In some job situations, this may not be a major issue; but in most you should have a carefully prepared explanation. The three-tier answer to difficult questions can be a useful tool here, since it enables you to soften the adverse effects of your situation. You should also try to convey that you were doing some consulting work during this period, as is commonly the case, and be able to present that as favorably as possible. Another useful thing may be to get a close friend in a responsible position to cover your time for you as much as possible. This is less important if you were ill.

**Lack of experience in your chosen field**

You may find yourself in a typical situation where you are trying to land a job which has five functional requirements and you have strong experience in four of them and very little in the fifth. For example, you may have been a chief financial officer with good overall experience but you have never had anything to do with selling your company's stock to the public for the first time. This might be a key requirement of a job you are being considered for.

First of all, to pursue the stock-selling example, you should identify the key elements needed to effectively carry out the function you lack experience in. Then from your experience in other functions, show that you have used many of the same skills in those key areas. For example, floating a stock issue requires such skills as dealing with investment bankers on the best strategy, timing and pricing, and dealing with lawyers and accountants on the technical aspects of the issue. Dealing with the investment bankers has many similarities to loans that you may have negotiated from banks and insurance companies.

Technical dealings with the lawyers and accountants are similar to a variety of activities that you have had in your job, such as making changes in the pension plan, dealing with financial regulations such as taxes, your annual audit, and so on. If you, in the past, have taken on a major role where you did not have much experience in the function and were able to overcome this experience deficiency fairly rapidly, emphasize that. Finally, you might find it necessary to improve your background in the field by hiring a consultant on a short-term basis.

For example, Paul Jones was the treasurer of a small company, where he was intimately involved with all the facets of the financial operation. He wanted to get big company experience in an important position. He located such a position which did not require high technical skills in a prestige company, but he needed experience in dealing with computer personnel. This was a function he had never been exposed to at all. To gain a working knowledge of computers, he hired a computer expert on a moonlighting basis. Jones met with this expert three or four evenings to discuss the kinds of things he would need to know about how a computer operated, how you communicate with computer personnel effectively, what you need out of the computer, and how you evaluate the procedures they set up. In a short time Jones was able to assimilate a basic understanding of computers so that he was able to get the job. Furthermore, he maintained a continuing relationship with the consultant, most of which was conducted by an occasional phone call, to get himself over the hurdle of day-to-day dealings with the computer. Jones not only got the job, but was able to handle it successfully.

**A confidential campaign**     You may want to look for a job while you are working and yet not burn the bridges on your present job. An effective method for conducting such a confidential campaign is outlined in Chapter Thirteen.

**Poor recent experience**

It is common for someone with a good record to make a job change and find that the new job and even possibly a second job doesn't work out. Ed Fisher learned to cope with this situation effectively (see p. 104).

**Lacking in-depth experience of your peers**

You may have had a long association with one company and worked up to a major position. You may find that your experience has been obtained in a company which is behind the times and therefore your skills aren't as strong as many individuals of your age and title competing in the market. If this is the case, you may have to take a step down in terms of title and salary in your new company. To minimize the possibility of this, your best opportunities probably are as a generalist rather than as a specialist. Your best bet is with smaller- or medium-sized companies.

**A mixed background**

Perhaps you have had a wide variety of experience (such as some marketing, some production, some administration) and are 10 or 15 years into your career without having a strong commitment to any single function. At this stage make it a top priority to identify what function you want to have for the rest of your career and find a job to get experience in it. The fact that you have had a mixture of experience may indicate real indecision on your part and very likely can work against you in the future.

Research should be the first step, so you can make a final choice of the function you want to pursue. To do this use the same technique as Gordon Sampson used in his career choice (see the section "Alternate Career Choices" in Chapter Three). This means selecting the two or three principal functional options and undergoing one to two months' intensive research whereby you can identify the pros and cons for each of these functions in terms of your basic interests and skills. In your case this may take considerably more time than for someone who is researching several career alternatives which are basically in his field (for example, selling, marketing, consulting, and so on). Having made your functional choice, prepare a job description of your preferred job. Then develop a functional resume to demonstrate the various experiences and skills in your background that are most favorable for the objective that you have (see Resume 6-10). You'll probably find that your choices are limited. With an aggressive and effective campaign, however, you should come up with several of them in time. If you find several job offers which meet a high standard for the function that you are anxious to get experience in, you will have taken a major step forward in furthering your career.

**A move to another location**

You may have decided to move to another location far distant from your current one. In doing this you have a key asset in the fact that most people want to be hospitable to a newcomer from another area. Used properly, you have an attribute which will allow you to open contacts at a much more rapid rate than you probably could in your home area. Tenuous affiliations from afar can develop rapidly into strong contacts.

Develop a key list of people to contact through such sources as your college alumni list for the area, trade association lists, and industry affiliations. Among your friends and associates in your current area are a number who may have contacts in your desired area. Most of them will be happy to provide an introduction for you. Don't minimize the value of such contacts. Harry Smith with many important contacts in his chosen new city almost didn't call a minister he was referred to.

When he did, he was introduced to a key member of the vestry who was vice chairman of one of the largest companies in the country. Within two weeks Harry was hired as vice president of a major subsidiary of this company.

The other key part of this strategy is to make your contacts in the new area from your home base. For example, a letter or a phone call written from Atlanta to an employer in Seattle is more likely to generate an interview than the same approach from the city of Seattle itself.

**Specialist in a declining industry**

Is your basic problem that you were a long-term career specialist in a technology or industry that is declining? If this is the case, try to identify the extent of the decline. If your industry is in a sharp, permanent decline and you have a long career ahead of you, it probably makes sense to face this situation now and make a change. If the decline is merely cyclical, and there has been a pattern of ups-and-downs for a long time, you have to ask yourself whether you want to put up with this for the rest of your life. If the number of jobs in your industry has declined substantially, staying in it means that you are going to have to conduct an intensive campaign and very likely make compromises on your immediate job goal. Perhaps you should seriously consider a change to a more promising industry (even though it may mean an immediate reduction in responsibilities and pay).

**Down-grading yourself**

You may have worked yourself up to a successful position earning $40,000 a year, but now perhaps find yourself looking for a job near the end of your career. Because you have held down a key job successfully at that salary, you may feel that merely indicating your willingness to accept a salary of say $25,000 should greatly expand your opportunities. It may or it may not. Visualize yourself as an employer hiring for a $25,000 position. You have to make a decision between two fairly equal candidates. One has been earning a $22,000 salary and the other was earning $40,000; wouldn't you as an employer be more inclined to the $22,000 candidate? To him or her it is a step forward, whereas for the $40,000 individual it would appear to be a step backward. You as the employer very likely may have the uneasy feeling that if another job comes up at a higher salary the latter will snap it up quickly.

If a large salary decrease is brought up by the employer and you are questioned about your feelings on it, here are some thoughts that you might use to convince an employer that some downgrading might be acceptable.

You may have been in a high risk or very demanding job and were paid a premium for it.

You may have been paid a high income but were given minimum fringe benefits so that your salary itself may seem higher than it actually was.

You may be very candid that your financial needs are much lower because your children are no longer living at home or being educated and your house is largely paid for.

At the same time develop the case that accepting a lower salary won't mean you're less motivated (that is because you'll be doing something you really want to do).

A key part of your strategy is approaching organizations which historically pay lower salaries than your latest one has. For example, smaller companies, nonprofit organizations, trade associations, and so on.

**Expert in a small, highly specialized industry**

An example of this is television advertising. A limited number of agencies and terrific competition for a few positions characterize this industry. Conduct a two-dimensional campaign: (*a*) a sophisticated one to the advertising firms and (b) a more general campaign to a wide variety of firms where your advertising and marketing skills can be used.

Unique to this type of campaign is the sophisticated approach to a few companies. You need to get as much background information on each company and its principals as possible, even though that might seem like overkill. Through research with people who work closely with a specific company (their media contacts, companies whose products they advertise, bankers, lawyers, and so on) find out the company's strengths and weaknesses, where it is putting particular current interest, the interests of the principals, and the like. This kind of industry is like a club—and good contacts and background information are most easily found by tapping into the grapevine. Then develop the best contact you possibly have to get to a key principal. Before you see him or her, however, carefully prepare a specialized approach related to most likely needs. Be persistent—while there's a lot of competition, much of it will get discouraged very quickly. Finally, approach as many companies as you can. Your general campaign—the second dimension—is in line with what has been described throughout this book—addressed to the advertising and marketing departments of a wide variety of organizations such as industrial and commercial companies, banks, and so on.

This chapter has covered a variety of job difficulties that often occur in an executive background. It obviously is not comprehensive. If you have a major problem that has not been covered, identify one or two problems addressed here that seem most comparable. Then try to use the same approaches that have been described in each of these sections.

# Chapter fifteen

# JOB HUNTING AND THE FAMILY

**Roles have changed**

Once upon a time, a person writing a book about executive job hunting addressed it to males—there were few if any women in that part of the job market. This is no longer the case. Today, women hold all kinds of executive positions, and this will be increasingly so. Women executives operate under the same pressures and frustrations as men, and they also look for jobs.

The principles and details on executive job hunting we have discussed apply equally to both sexes. And the stresses and strains job hunting lays on the family are similar whether a husband or a wife is looking. In the past, a wife's job was almost always in the home; she had no need to job hunt. Her role was to support and aid the husband who searched. In some families now, those roles have switched. Moreover, a large number of women carry on jobs while raising a family without a husband around.

All this is introductory to a discussion of the family's role in job hunting. "Family" here can mean the nuclear—wife and husband, or those together with children. It can also mean a single parent and children—and there are more and more instances in which the single parent is a man. The main point is that job hunting—by a wife, a husband, or a single parent—affects the family, and the family in turn affects the job hunter and the task.

**What the family goes through**

The loss of a job threatens a family's security and future, whether that job represents the sole source of income or not. It has an impact on a family's relations with friends and the community in general. And this condition prevails until a job hunt ends successfully.

For a two-income family the situation is not catastrophic, but it is tough nonetheless. For an indefinite period the family must cut back, but this is more easily stated than accomplished, especially if the family is bearing such heavy obligations as college tuition. For the single-income family, the situation might call for the other spouse to find employment temporarily—assuming the person has a marketable skill—with all the stresses and strains that entails.

A period of job searching is one in which the family must draw together, perhaps as never before, to support the person directly involved. And this refers to children as well as to husband and wife. Discussions should be open and candid, and all should be involved in decisions.

In this chapter we look at the situation from two standpoints—the job hunter's and that of the other spouse. Despite rapid changes in our culture, where a nuclear family is involved, most typically the job hunter is the husband. I'll assume that here, not for any sexist reason, but simply for purposes of illustration. Male and female roles considered here could be reversed. Keep that in mind.

**The
job-hunting
husband**

First of all, you probably feel guilty, at fault for bringing this state of affairs on your family. The large number of reasons for being out of work that attach no blame to the person, and the huge number of people in your situation at any one time, do not impress you. The main thing is that it has happened to you, and you can't help reflecting that had you done something differently you wouldn't be in this predicament. Perhaps, perhaps not. In any case, that is irrelevant. The important thing now is to find another job. To feel guilty is normal, but it is a luxury you can't afford to wallow in for long. Life is real, so sooner rather than later get to the task at hand.

Since you're probably the principal breadwinner, you should consider the effect of your job search on your family, particularly your wife. The decision you make, especially if it involves a geographic move, can have a dramatic effect on her life. It could be a threat to all she holds most dear—your home, her friends, her career and community involvements. She may not volunteer her concerns, recognizing the tremendous pressure you're under. Tell her you understand and appreciate her support.

You may have a strong tendency to keep things to yourself at this time. You're having a rough enough time as it is. To bring in your wife and children, you feel, might put limits on acceptable jobs, making things more difficult than they already are. This is a normal—even though shortsighted—attitude. Your fears can outdistance reality.

If you don't involve your wife, and your children—especially if they're teenagers, they may resist your accepting a job they perceive is adverse to their interests. Discuss fears with them all. Listen to them. Try to understand them. Usually it is particularly upsetting if a new job might require a

move. You might explain: "The last thing I want to
do is move to such and such. On the other hand,
the implications of no job at all (or a much lower
paying job) are even worse—on our living standard,
plans for college, and so on." You may also want
to make the point that looking for a job at this
stage in your career is the hardest thing you've ever
had to do.

Discuss all aspects of the situation with your
family. Talk about the kind of job you want and
the task of finding it. Ask for their support and
opinions.

Your wife knows you better than anybody else
does, and she often can provide constructive insight. Some of her goals may be different from
yours, and you should get the matter of goals out
in the open and discuss them at the start. There
would be nothing worse than for you to make a
major decision without your wife's general agreement. Not only would this mean additional pressure on your marriage, but it could also be a major
stumbling block to success in your new job.

You may have sheltered your wife from your
financial situation—this, unfortunately, is more
common than you might think. If you have, you
no longer can conceal financial realities. And share
this information with your children. If nothing
else, to do so is to show respect and it will help to
reinforce their support. They probably will volunteer to carry an additional load at home and realize
that, at least for a time, they must give up costly
things that they have been looking forward to—
such as going to camp.

Unless you are unusual, your normal bills to
maintain your current standard of living have con-
sumed most of your family income. You all may be
concerned about how to pay for next week's gro-
ceries. When you projected your expenses for a
campaign of reasonable length, you probably

assured yourself that while the immediate financial situation when you are unemployed would not be strong, it would be aided by reduced taxes, and possibly supplemented by severance pay and unemployment compensation (see the section on financial management in Chapter Two). It is very much to your advantage that your family get a realistic picture of your finances, and you should all beware of the pressure that might build up to take the first job that comes along mainly for financial reasons, even though it isn't suitable.

Your family can help you with certain details of job hunting. For example, if your wife types she can be a great asset.

You and your wife might talk with other couples who have been through the job-hunting process. What did they learn that was useful in coping?

This is a time when you particularly need emotional outlets. Don't give up on your other personal interests (community activities, athletics, and hobbies). On the other hand, don't let them infringe on time you should be job hunting.

**The wife**

Now let's turn to your situation from your wife's point-of-view. It's important that she read the book, and this section in particular. It will make her much more aware of what you're going through. This will help her understand it and deal with it, and enable her to be more helpful to you. Let's talk about Mary McGuinn for awhile.

A short time ago, life seemed blissful—comparatively. Mary McGuinn's husband had a good job—he was a respected member of the community—and she enjoyed a positive identity. And now, through whatever quirk of fate, the picture has changed greatly. Her husband is without a job—and thus a great uncertainty has crept into her future. It may be months before he gets a new

job—it may not pay as much or be as prestigious as
the last one—the family may have to move to another area.

Little wonder Mary's apprehensive and frustrated, and she feels she's lost prestige. She's probably even downright mad! Why did this have to
happen to her, and through no fault of her own?
Particularly when she was on the brink of doing
some things that she had worked hard for—an addition to the house, a really special vacation, doing
something for the children she'd always wanted to.

But what has happened is a fact of life! And
nothing Mary can do is going to change it. But
more than any other person besides her husband,
she can turn this adversity into something positive—something which three years from now will
make the current period what it is: a temporary
setback. After all, for an average man, for how
much time out of a working career of 40-plus years
is he likely to be out of work?

Besides, was the last job really that great? What
about the time Mary's husband was ready for a big
promotion and it went to somebody less qualified?
Or the big project her husband worked hard on,
only to have somebody else get the credit? Remember the long hours, the traveling, the small
raise after such a long wait?

The loss of a job is devastating—but a lot worse
things could have happened to Mary. The death
or disablement of her husband, or the loss, disfig-
urement, or permanent incapacitation of a child.
These are permanent—the loss of job is temporary.

Not so many months ago Mary was proud of her
husband's accomplishments and reputation. She
thought nothing could raise doubts about them.
Well, there are still no real doubts. Those skills and
fine qualities are still there, and they will undoubtedly be strengthened in the competitive process
he's going through. He will emerge a bit scarred by
his experience perhaps, but a wiser, more mature,

and more realistic person—and that's to their mutual benefit in the highly competitive world we live in. Literally millions of successful people have been through a job hunt well along in their careers, and they have emerged stronger people because of it. And this process has affected people at all levels—no one is immune. Mary and her husband face frustrations and concerns common to millions.

Another thing: since Mary's husband started his career, there really hasn't been a practical opportunity to get out of the rat race. And this is doubly true when he was in a job that was going along pretty well. But Mary and her husband now have an opportunity to get out, if they choose, without the difficulty of having to make the decision to give up a good job. Regardless of what they do, they have the opportunity to take a good look at themselves and decide whether some of the "necessities" which have crept into their lives are really that important. It may mean, if the family chooses, a job with less pressure, a reasonably secure future, and more time together.

Most friends don't know what they can do to help—and yet they want to and will rally when called on. Further, Mary will be gratified by some of the things some will do spontaneously—often people whom she wouldn't expect to respond. This is real support—and if she does need help, most will react in a positive way.

**A word to all wives**

Now for a few thoughts addressed to all the Mary McGuinns of the world.

1. Your husband may be going through a more difficult experience than ever before. He's getting rejected on almost a daily basis. He has feelings of letting his family down. He may have feelings of guilt for having lost his job—even though that could have happened to anyone in his position. He needs your total support—and nobody else can give him the help you can! Let him know that

you're proud of him and that you appreciate everything he has done and what he is doing now. Remember he's out there working for the family too.

2. He needs someone before whom he can let his hair down—someone who will really listen and understand. He'll have his ups and downs, more so probably than when he had a job. Something that looked good one day will disappear overnight! Often he won't want to talk about how things are going—but you're being there ready can be a great source of comfort. If he has an inclination to talk, listen. He needs someone he can let it all out to.

3. A key to your husband's success in his job search is a high level of self-confidence. It's inevitable that at times during the campaign it will be at a low ebb. Give him all the encouragement you can.

4. You may have certain doubts about your husband's ability or his judgment. Be careful here. He is probably looking to you as his greatest booster. There may be occasions when you can subtly call his attention to certain limitations in a constructive way.

5. You need to give vent to your frustrations. In many ways you're under more pressure than anyone. Under the circumstances, you won't find it easy to let off steam to your husband. Seek out a friend. You may find that a wife whose husband went through a long job search may be particularly helpful. Not only may she be more understanding than many friends, but she may have some constructive suggestions.

6. In the past you may have put pressure on your husband to strive beyond his abilities or inclinations. If you feel his goal is too high, let him know that you and the family support him if he chooses a more limited objective.

7. It's important that all of your children, especially the older, be brought into the picture—so they can cope with the family uncertainty in their

own ways. It may affect their personal plans (for example, college or a summer camp deferred). It may affect their schoolwork. You are in the best position to allay their fears.

8. You should be sensitive to the fact that it is often difficult for you to help your husband. But it's often difficult for spouses to achieve objectivity and to set emotions aside. You may be surprised to find that your husband has goals for his life that perhaps you were completely unaware of. These can be things that are very personal and deep-seated, and that he never has really talked about. They could be such things as a compulsive striving for success, or a desire to make a lot of money or to strive for a very prestigious image. These may not be important to you as goals for him, but to him they may be very real. If his motivations toward these goals are intense, you may be powerless to dissuade him from them. Get him to talk to somebody he particularly admires. That person may be able to make him understand that his goals are unrealistic—if they are—and get him to be more practical. He may need personal job counseling help, or even possibly psychological help. Here again a person that he particularly respects may be able to persuade him to this.

9. The strain on you may be just as great—or even greater than on your husband. You need to get rid of your frustrations in the same way your husband does. But both of you must be careful not to vent your frustrations on each other.

10. You may be tempted at this time to load your husband with a lot of the household chores. That's normal. Perhaps he can share the load more. But don't be tempted to push him into doing a lot that takes time from his job campaign. That's his and your first priority! And it's a full-time, high-pressure job. Detracting him from it will only prolong the frustration of his being out of work or it may lead him to accept a job you'll both regret.

# Chapter sixteen

# WHERE DO YOU GO FROM HERE?

**Pressures of transition**

You've received a satisfactory offer and you've accepted it. You may be one of the fortunate who have accepted "the job you've really been looking for" or, like many, you accepted the best you could get—it's acceptable, but you have reservations—or you may be in between. If you are at the lower end of the scale in terms of satisfaction with your choice, you may be the more fortunate—because perhaps you are the one being most realistic about the new job. Whatever the case, you're over the first of two main hurdles in changing jobs— landing the position.

Before you lies a different kind of challenge and one just as important to the job-change process— adjusting to the new job. Your indoctrination may go well—I hope it does—but it constitutes another period of emotional pressure. Your new challenge will be exciting, but it also can be traumatic. You'll be adjusting to a new company which has different ways of doing things. You'll find some things you didn't or couldn't anticipate, and your performance will be closely watched not only by your boss but by the organization as a whole. For a short period of time most people will probably go out of their way to be helpful, but eventually the honeymoon will end.

There may be unusual upset in your family. If the new job means a change to a new location, it could unsettle everyone, particularly teen-age children. Even if the job doesn't involve a move, it still can mean upset to your family (different hours, greater pressures, more traveling, sometimes reduced salary, and so on). All of this puts additional pressure on you over and above the problems of getting settled in the new position.

The best way to prepare for all this is to take time off. You and the whole family deserve it. If your job search was a long one, try to have a vacation away from home. It may seem a poor time to do so financially, but it will enable you to begin the new job refreshed and relaxed. A couple of weeks away will give you all a chance to catch your breath. If you can't travel, just a couple of weeks at home doing the things that you like to do could be a real help in making a successful transition.

**Getting acclimated**

The next step is to make the job a success. One of the more sophisticated screening processes for selecting people for key positions is the professional draft of various professional athletes. Certainly it is one of the important factors in a team's future success. Each team has highly trained people scouting prospects, developing the most sophisticated statistics on each player's attributes, computerizing the information, and extensively observing movies of individuals. Yet the results are quite spotty. Often first-round draft choices don't even make the squad, while players at the bottom of the draft list, walk-ons, or players cut from other teams, turn out to be stars. One reason for this mixed bag of success is the use of poor judgment on the part of the screeners, but a key part is the determination of the players. Often the difference between those who are marginal but make the squad and those who are considered shoe-ins and don't, is that the former psych themselves up so that they are absolutely determined to make the team, whereas those who fail are not so well motivated. Before you start your new job, develop the determination that you are going to make it a success at all costs. And at this time you have a lot going for you. When you come aboard, your boss and the others involved in your hiring want you to be a success—by hiring you they placed their reputations on the line.

Your first objective is to win the confidence of the people who are keys to your success on the job. You should have become a better salesman of yourself in the job-hunting process, since you convinced key people in the organization to make you a good offer. On the other hand your coming on board creates some problems—you may be a threat to the future aspirations of others, you may be looked upon as someone who got a job they felt they deserved, you may have taken over duties that someone considered his or hers, or you may be getting rewards or benefits others don't have or didn't get so quickly. So you have a new type of selling job to do—to affirm to the key people that they made the right choice, and to win the acceptance of the others. The selling techniques of really listening to your associates' needs and responding to them are your best tools. Several other skills that you probably have improved considerably in your job search are key management tools on any job. For example:

Producing good work in a highly competitive environment.

Communicating effectively (in writing, on the phone, and in interviewing).

Dealing with emotional upset.

Identifying your weaknesses and overcoming them.

Being self-disciplined.

Managing your time.

Developing and working toward specific goals.

You may find it worthwhile to think about what skills you improved in your job search and how they can be useful in the new job. At the same time, you have identified some weaknesses that need working on for the future.

Here are some guiding thoughts for you at this stage.

First, keep a low profile. During the hiring process, and probably in the late stages of it, you were exposed to top management, individuals with whom you may not have a close relationship on the job. At that time they were trying to hire you, so they rolled out the red carpet. Don't overdo your relationship with them, until you are involved with them on the job. Trying to play a role with them that is not realistic may turn them off, and it may antagonize people you have to deal with on a regular basis.

Second, while you are in the first few weeks of the job, try to sit down and talk at length with the key people your job relates to—obviously your boss, but also your key subordinates and peers to whom you relate in other parts of the company. Try not to prejudge their needs. But ask a lot of questions about how your role relates to theirs and what kind of things you can do to help them. Try to get some understanding of the climate in which they operate, and also the climate in which solutions to problems are made. Find out what their ideas are on solutions to the problems. Be an alert listener and watch what you say. To point out that "this is the way we solved your problem at XYZ" is a fast way to lose rapport with your new associates. They will naturally think that the problems that exist at your new company are much different from those at XYZ, yet naturally what you did at XYZ in solving similar problems probably got you the job. But in most cases the persons you are talking to have thought of this solution. Maybe it has been tried and didn't work. Before you suggest any solution, try to find out what have been the real roadblocks and what is necessary to overcome them.

Third, be ready for surprises—there are bound to be some. There are subtle relationships in any organization that are inherent to it. Undoubtedly there were things you were not told which have an important bearing on your job and things you were told which you may have misunderstood. Be observant and perceptive on how the surprises are likely to affect you, and act accordingly.

Fourth, don't be nosy. In time you will learn the things you'll need to know. You'll learn more of them as you win the confidence of key people.

Fifth, you may find yourself lacking technical knowledge of a function in your area. If it is important for you, and it involves expertise that you are not likely to be able to pick up as quickly as needed, hire a consultant. (See Chapter Fourteen, "Lack of Experience in Your Chosen Field.")

Sixth, in general it makes sense to "play the game" as it exists in the organization. When you have established a strong power base, then you can deviate from that plan to the extent feasible. Your success on the job depends mainly on your relationship with your boss. A principal part of your efforts should be in satisfying his or her needs. Analyze what they are (and the pressures your boss is subjected to) and try within the context of your responsibility to satisfy them. It's easy to get embroiled in what you are doing (that is, what you're interested in or what you think is needed) and lose perspective on the most important things you can do for your boss. Develop good communications— be sure what you are really doing is understood and that you are effectively carrying out his or her interests. Observe what your boss's hang-ups are— not only in dealings with you, but with others. Conduct yourself so that you aren't in conflict with them.

Wherever you go within the organization, you are your boss's representative—make sure you are a good one. On the other hand, you want to be cautious to not be completely identified with your boss, because his or her star may fall, and yours with it.

**Outside offers**

Other offers might emerge as a result of your campaign. What you do about them is a matter of judgment, timing, and how the new job is going. If an inquiry about a particularly attractive job comes up, it may make sense to consider it. Certainly don't reject it without one or two days' thought, because once rejected it is gone. Be extremely cautious in handling other job possibilities that appear right after you start a new job. The worst thing that could happen would be to lose your new job or to find yourself under a cloud in its early stages. Any indication that you're not satisfied at this time comes when you've established little permanent rapport, so you may not be given the benefit of the doubt.

**Plan for the future**

You have already seen that many of the skills developed in your job campaign are useful in getting acclimated to the job. Obviously many of these skills have just as much value in the long run.

After you have your job under control, start planning for the future. Decide where you would like to be 5 or 10 years hence.

A useful starting place is the list of job requirements that you prepared in Chapter Three, What Do You Want to Do? Having decided on your goal, define the functional experience and skills you will probably need to attain it. Next analyze what you have to do to develop this experience and these skills. This development plan will consist of:

Specific job experience that you need.

The courses that you should take and seminars you should attend.

The types of contacts you should try to make (for example, through trade associations).

Reading what you should do.

One or two key community activities, provided they don't infringe on your job performance (for example, if you are a controller, and you would like to get some marketing experience, it might be useful for you to run a substantial fund drive—such as the annual drive of your church).

Can a consultant speed up this learning process?

What personal characteristics and skills particularly need strengthening? How can you best develop them?

Once you have determined the experience you want, lay out a program for getting it. Then implement this program with a carefully prepared schedule. "The Failure Analysis Tool" explained in Chapter Eleven, Building and Maintaining Momentum, can be helpful in scheduling such a program. To make your plan effective, periodically review your progress against it. Monthly, semiannual, and annual reviews should suffice. At the end of each year record your principal accomplishments, not only for the development plan but as basic material if and when you have to conduct another job campaign. And periodically update your resume. The process of doing so will force you to evaluate your progress from a somewhat different standpoint. It may also remind you of the key skills you are not currently using, but which can some way be used.

Finally, review your financial status. As I pointed out in Chapter Two, Avoid the Traps, the financial drain probably has not been as great as you might have expected. A key part of your plan for the future is to develop a financial reserve for the possibility of having to make another job change.

**If your new job fails**

By now you are familiar with the great risk in any new job. Even though you may have put on a good job campaign, you may find that the job is nowhere near as good as you thought it would be. What should you do? Make another job search or bite the bullet? Some of the ideas in Chapter Thirteen, Should You Make a Job Change—If You Have a Choice? may be useful, although that chapter was written primarily for people who have been on a job for quite some time.

If you find out almost immediately that you've made an error in accepting the job you did, there are several additional possibilities. You may want to reopen discussions with companies which made offers that you refused. In addition you may still have some momentum from your campaign and several possibilities may come up in your first few months on the new job. Your best bet, though, may be to meet the problem head-on. By this I mean you might approach your boss and lay the cards on the table, suggesting that you phase out of the company over a period of several months and switch from a salary to a consulting (for example, per diem) basis. This will provide a means of covering up this mistake in your future job search.

If neither of these solutions seems practical, and you decide to make a change, carefully plan when to do it. Ultimately only you can answer this question, but careful consideration can help minimize your emotional reaction and thus facilitate making a sound decision. What is an acceptable time frame with a loser job? This is a time to be really conservative. A period of a few months on a job can look very poor on your record. In addition, it will not be easy to put on a new job campaign since you have just been through one unsuccessfully. Your friends and contacts will help, but much less enthusiastically than they did before. Your finances are probably in poor shape at the moment. Therefore, recognizing that your career will probably span 40 years or more, spending a year or two on this job may be best in the long run. If you decide to do this, do it with a commitment to a maximum effort to develop yourself for the future as much as you can on the job. Coping with a bad job situation and learning how to make it better can be a valuable experience. No matter how good your next job is, you will run into periods when it doesn't seem to be going well. Being more effective in coping with this condition can be a help to you.

Also ask yourself which of your goals are possibly achievable while you are with your current company, and which aren't. Then make a strong effort to reach the achievable goals. They may be useful in minimizing the effect of the black mark of a one- or two-year tenure on a poor job.

## Conclusion

If your campaign has been successful, let's hope it's been constructive in terms of your long-term future. Your job campaign has forced you to examine your long-term goals in depth, and it should have resulted in a job in line with them. Many of your peers may seem fortunate in that they have not had to go through this process. On the other hand, they may find themselves "locked in" to jobs that they're not particularly happy with and that don't promise the futures they'd like. Also in your campaign you have sharpened some old skills and learned some new ones which may be useful the rest of your life. Above all other things, you should have learned that you can control your career to a much greater extent than you realized before. You also should have emerged from your campaign a different person—more realistic, better directed, and more effective. Undoubtedly it hasn't been an easy time. But a really good job for you at this stage of your career can provide you with one of the greatest satisfactions of your life.

Good luck and good hunting!